Contents

Introduction

PART 1-PENSIONS

PART 2-GENERAL FINANCIAL ISSUES

PART 3-FINANCE AND INVESTMENTS

STRAIGHTFORWARD GUIDE TO PLANNING FOR RETIREMENT

MANAGING RETIREMENT FINANCES

PATRICK GRANT

Editor: Roger Sproston

Straightforward Publishing
www.straightforwardco.co.uk

Straightforward Guides

© Straightforward Co Ltd 2021

ISBN
978-1-913776-50-3

Printed by 4Edge Ltd www.4Edge.co.uk

Cover design by Straightforward Graphics

Introduction

Enjoying a fruitful and prosperous retirement is the goal of most people, yet when the day finally arrives quite often the finances necessary to ensure a peaceful old age are just not there. There are many reasons for this, the most common being lack of adequate planning in the earlier, more productive years. In addition, lack of knowledge of exactly what is on offer for those who have reached retirement age, such as the range of benefits available, along with other age related benefits also contributes to the relative poverty of today's retirees. The changes in pension provisions also mean that people, particularly women, have to wait longer for their pensions.

COVID 19

Along with everyone else, people approaching retirement age have been affected by the Pandemic. This has had an effect on finances and future care along with holidays and just about every aspect of life. At the time of writing we are approaching the end of restrictions and hopefully life will return to a semblance of normality.

The aim of this book, updated to **2021**, is to explain, in as much depth as possible, the workings of the pension industry, how you can maximise your pension before retiring, and also how to take care of other fundamental areas of life such as planning for care and maintaining good health. There is a new section on savings, insurance and investing in the stock market. There is also a chapter on identifying and dealing with fraud.

The emphasis of this book is, as the title states, on the planning and management of finances following retirement, and ensuring that all areas of life which require financial know how and management are explored. The book covers pensions, continuing to work, taxation, health and care and also the management of your home. We all want to enjoy our retirement in peace and be relatively prosperous. It is hoped that this book will at least provide a stepping-stone to this end.

Patrick Grant
2021

PART 1
PENSIONS

Ch. 1

Pensions-Planning for the Future

Planning for the future

The main principle with all pension provision is that the sooner you start saving money in a pension plan the more you will have at retirement. The later that you leave it the less you will have or the more expensive that it will be to create a fund adequate enough for your needs. The following chapters outline pensions and sources of pensions in detail. It may be that, if you are already retired you cannot take advantage of certain pension schemes, such as occupational pensions. However, if you are looking at your various options before retirement then the information should prove useful.

In order to gauge your retirement needs, you will need to have a clear idea of your lifestyle, or potential lifestyle in retirement. This is not something that you can plan, or want to plan, at a younger age but the main factor is that the more that you have the easier life will be. There are two main factors which currently underpin retirement:

- Improved health and longevity-we are living longer and we have better health so therefore we are more active
- People are better off-improved state and company pensions

Sources of pension and other retirement income

Government statistics indicate that there is a huge gap between the poorest and richest pensioners in the United Kingdom. No surprise there. The difference between the richest fifth of single pensioners and the poorest fifth is about £400 per week. The poorest fifth of pensioners in the UK are reliant mainly on state benefits whilst the wealthier groups have occupational incomes and also personal investment incomes. The outline below indicates sources of pension and also the disparity between the richest and poorest socio-economic groups:

The Pensioners Income Series

The Pensioners' Incomes (PI) Series contains estimates of the levels, sources and distribution of pensioners' incomes. It also examines the position of pensioners within the income distribution of the population as a whole. This can be found at:

www.gov.uk/government/collections/pensioners-incomes-series.

Average income of pensioners

The figures show that the median weekly income for single pensioners is £285 (2021/22), down from £312 in the 2012-13 tax year. Income earned by retired workers is made up of several sources including the state pension, workplace pensions, personal pensions and income from savings and investments.

Pensioners need £33,000 for a comfortable retirement moneyfacts.co.uk In order for workers to enjoy a comfortable retirement that includes holidays abroad, a generous clothing

10

allowance and a car they will need to have saved enough for a £33,000 per year income.

Couples tend to have more retirement income than single people. Some reports even suggest that in 2017/18, retired couples received more than twice the income of single retirees. This may partly be due to the fact that housing costs were included in the study – couples sharing housing will generally have lower overheads than someone on their own. Another factor may be that those who are single upon entering retirement are likely to be divorced or separated, which may have had a significant impact on their past finances and thus their ability to save for retirement. People in long-term stable relationships may have a greater capacity for building up retirement funds, as well as a stronger motivation for doing so.

Sources of pensioner incomes

Nearly all pensioners (97 per cent) were in receipt of the State Pension in 2021/22. Income-related benefits were received by a quarter of all pensioners in 2019/20. The percentage of pensioners in receipt of income-related benefits has decreased from 34 per cent in 2005/06 to 25 per cent in 2021/22. This has been influenced by the increase in the State Pension and the targeting of Pension Credit on the pensioners on lowest incomes.

There has been little change in the percentage of pensioners with income from disability benefits. This income category covers a range of benefits paid to individuals as a result of their disability status.

Personal pensions provide income to a smaller group of pensioners than occupational pensions. The percentage of

11

pensioners in receipt has increased over a 10 year period. In 2021/22, 18 per cent of pensioners were in receipt of income from personal pensions, compared with 12 per cent in 2005/06. Recently retired pensioners were more likely to be in receipt than older pensioners, which reflects the relatively recent expansion in the numbers contributing to personal pensions. Personal pensions in their current form were introduced in 1988.

Private pension income includes all non-State Pension income. Over the past 10 years, there has been an increase in the percentage of pensioners receiving income from private pensions – from 66 per cent to 70 per cent. Investment income was the third most common source of income, received by 63 per cent of all pensioners in 2021/22 although the percentage of pensioners in receipt of investment income has decreased from 70 per cent over the past 10 years. Overall 17 per cent of pensioners were in receipt of earnings. Some of the results for pensioner couples include earnings from one person being under State Pension age.

Pensioners income according to position-bottom fifth of pensioners and top fifth

Benefit income, including State Pension income, was the largest source of income for both single pensioners and couples in the bottom fifth of the income distribution. For pensioner couples in this group benefit income accounted for 78 per cent of their income, while for single pensioners this was 86 per cent. Benefit income made up more than half of all income for all but the top fifth of single pensioners.

For the top fifth of both couples and singles, the largest source of income was from private pension income (38 per cent for couples and 44 per cent for singles). For couples the proportion of income from earnings was highest in the top fifth of the income distribution.

Amongst other things, the above illustrates that those in the poorest and wealthiest bands have a wide gap in income, in particular in the areas of earnings and investments. The richest have managed to ensure that there is enough money in the pot to cater for retirement. Those in the lower income bands rely heavily on state pensions and other benefits. The Pensioners Income Series measures those within the bottom, middle and top fifth of the population.

How Much Income is needed in Retirement-Planning Ahead

When attempting to forecast for future pension needs, there are a number of factors which need to be taken into account: These are:

- Your income needs in retirement and how much of that income you can expect to derive from state pensions
- How much pension that any savings you have will produce
- How long you have to save for
- Projected inflation

Income needs in retirement

This is very much a personal decision and will be influenced by a number of factors, such as ongoing housing costs, care costs, projected lifestyle etc. The main factor is that you have enough to live on comfortably. In retirement you will probably take more

13

holidays and want to enjoy your free time. This costs money so your future planning should take into account all your projected needs and costs. When calculating future needs, all sources of income should be taken into account.

What period to save over

The obvious fact is that, the longer period that you save over the more you will build up and hence the more that you will have in retirement. As time goes on savings are compounded and the value of the pot goes up. One thing is for certain and that is if you leave it too late then you will have to put away a large slice of your income to produce a decent pension. If you plan to retire at an early age then you will need to save more to produce the same benefits.

Inflation

As prices rise, so your money buys you less. This is the main effect of inflation and to maintain the same level of spending power you will need to save more as time goes on. Many forms of retirement plans will include a calculation for inflation. Currently, inflation is at a relatively low level. However, history shows that the effects of inflation can be corrosive, having risen above 25% per annum in the past. Hopefully, this is now under control

For most people, retirement is a substantial part of life, probably lasting a couple of decades or more. It follows that ensuring your financial security in retirement requires some forward planning. Developing a plan calls for a general review of your current finances and careful consideration of how you can build up your savings to generate the retirement income that you need.

There are five distinct stages to planning your retirement which are summarised below.

Stage 1-this involves checking first that other aspects of your basic finances are in good shape. Planning for retirement generally means locking away your money for a long time. Once invested it is usually impossible to get pension savings back early, even in an emergency. It is therefore essential that you have other more accessible savings available for emergencies and that you do not have any problem debts that could tip you into a financial crisis. You must then weigh up saving for retirement against other goals that are more pressing, such as making sure that your household would be financially secure if you were unable to work because of illness or the main breadwinner dies.

Stage 2-You need to decide how much income you might need when you retire. There is a table overleaf which might help you in calculating this.
Stage 3- Check how much pension that you have built up so far.
Stage 4-Compare your amount from stage 3 with your target income from stage 2.
Stage 5-Review your progress once a year and/or if your circumstances change.

It is a fact that many people need far less in retirement than when actively working. The expenses that exist when working, such as mortgage payments, children and work related expenses do not exist when retired. The average household between 30-49 spends

£473 per week and £416 between 50-64. This drops to £263 per week between 65 to 74 and even lower in later retirement (Expenditure and Food Survey).

However, as might be expected, expenditure on health care increases correspondingly with age. Whilst the state may help with some costs the individual still has to bear a high proportion of expenditure on health related items. When calculating how much money you will need in retirement, it is useful to use a table in order to list your anticipated expenses as follows

Everyday needs

Item	Annual Total
Food and other	
Leisure (newspapers etc)	
Pets	
Clothes	
Other household items	
Gardening	
General expenses	

Home expenses

Mortgage/rent	
Service charges/repairs	
Insurance	
Council tax	
Water and other utilities	
Telephone	

TV licence other charges (satellite)	
Other expenses (home help)	

Leisure and general entertainment

Hobbies	
Eating out	
Cinema/theatre	
Holidays	
Other luxuries (smoking/drinking	

Transport

Car expenses	
Car hire	
Petrol etc	
Bus/train fares	

Health

Dental charges	
Optical expenses	
Medical insurance	
Care insurance	
Other health related expenses	

Anniversaries/birthdays etc

Children/grandchildren	
Relatives other than children	
Christmas	
Charitable donations	
Other expenses	

Savings and loans

General savings	
Saving for later retirement	
Other savings	
Loan repayments	

Other

The above should give you an idea of the amounts that you will need per annum to live well. Obviously, you should plan for a monthly income that will meet those needs. You should also take account of income tax on your retirement incomes.

****

Chapter 2

Sources of Pensions-A Summary

For certain, one area that people should be thinking about as they approach retirement is the amount of income they will need to live on and what they will actually get. The state pension is a reliable source of income. However, it is almost certain that a person will need more than this.

The state pension

Over 96% of single pensioners and 99% of couples receive the basic state pension. Therefore, it is here to stay. Everyone who has paid the appropriate national insurance contributions will be entitled to a state pension. If you are not working you can either receive pension credits, as discussed, or make voluntary contributions.

The full (basic) state pension is £134.24 for a single person (2020) From April 2021, for men who were born after 6th April 1951 and women who were born after 6th April 1953 the pension is £179.60 per week. This is known as a 'flat rate' or 'single tier' system and is designed to make the current system more simple and easier to understand. Getting the flat rate however, is very much dependant on contributions.

Basic state pensions are increased each April in line with price inflation. State pensioners also receive a (£10 Christmas bonus-check current entitlement) and are entitled to winter fuel payments. Married women can claim a pension based on their

19

spouse's NI record. Men who have reached 65 are also able to claim a basic state pension based on their wife's contribution record where the wife reaches state pension age on or after 6th April 2010.

Same sex couples, as a result of the Civil Partnerships Act 2004, along with married couples of the same sex, following the passing of the Marriage (Same sex Couples Act) 2014, have the same rights as heterosexual couples in all aspects of pension provision.

Transsexual people

Your State Pension might be affected if you're a transsexual person and you:

- were born between 24 December 1919 and 3 April 1945
- were claiming State Pension before 4 April 2005
- can provide evidence that your gender reassignment surgery took place before 4 April 2005

You don't need to do anything if you legally changed your gender and started claiming State Pension on or after 4 April - you'll already be claiming based on your legal gender. For more details go to www.gov.uk/state-pension/eligibility

How many qualifying years do you need to get the full State Pension?

The number of qualifying years you need to get a full state pension depends on when you reach your State Pension age. If you reached State Pension age before 6 April 2010, you normally needed 44 qualifying years if you are a man, or 39 qualifying years if you are woman. If you reach State Pension age on or after 6 April 2010 but before 6 April 2016, you need 30 qualifying years. If you reach State Pension age on or after 6 April 2016, you normally need 35 qualifying years.

Using someone else's contribution record

In some circumstances, you may be able to use your husband's, wife's or civil partner's contribution record to help you qualify for a State Pension.

Pension credits

Pension credits began life in October 2003. The credit is designed to top up the resources of pensioners whose income is low. The pension credit has two components: a guarantee credit and a saving credit.

The Guarantee credit

This is available to anyone over a qualifying age (equal to women's state pension age-see further on) whose income is less than a set amount called the minimum guarantee. The guarantee will bring income up to £177.10 for a single personand £270.30 for a couple (including civil partners and ame ex couples) (2021-2022). The minimum guarantee is higher for ertain categories of disabled people and carers. The qualifying ge or Pension Credit is gradually going up to 66 in line with the ncrease in the State Pension age for women to 65 and the urther ncrease to 66 for men and women.**The Savings credit**You can only claim savings credit if you or your partner are aged 65 or over. It's intended as a modest "reward" if you've provided yourself with a retirement income over and above the basic retirement pension.Savings credit is calculated by the The maximum savings credit you can get is £14.04 a week if you're

21

single and £15.71 a week if you're married or living with a partner.

The income taken into account for savings credit is the same as for guarantee credit, but various types of income are now ignored. These are Working Tax Credit, contribution-based Employment and Support Allowance, Incapacity Benefit, contribution-based Jobseeker's Allowance, Severe Disablement Allowance, Maternity Allowance and maintenance payments made to you (child maintenance is always ignored).

If your income is still over the savings threshold, the Pension Service works out your entitlement to savings credit.

If you reach State Pension age on or after 6 April 2016

Most people who reach State Pension age on or after 6 April 2016 won't be eligible for Savings Credit. But you may continue to get Savings Credit if both of the following apply:

- you're in a couple and one of you reached State Pension age before 6 April 2016
- you were getting Savings Credit up to 6 April 2016
- If you stop being eligible for Savings Credit for any reason from 6 April 2016, you won't be able to get it again.

National Insurance Credits

In some situations you may get National Insurance Credits, which plug what would otherwise be gaps in your NI record. You might get credits in the following situations:

- when you are unemployed, or unable to work   because you are ill, and claiming certain benefits
- If you were aged 16 to 18 before 6 April 2010, you were usually credited automatically with National Insurance credits. No new awards will be made from 6 April 2010.

- if you are on an approved training course
- when you are doing jury service
- if you are getting Statutory Adoption Pay, Statutory Maternity Pay, Additional Statutory Paternity Pay, Statutory Sick Pay, Maternity Allowance or Working Tax Credit
- if you have been wrongly put in prison
- if you are caring for a child or for someone who is sick or disabled
- if you are aged 16 or over and provided care for a child under 12, that you are related to and you lived in the UK for the period(s) of care
- if your spouse or civil partner is a member of Her Majesty's forces and you are accompanying them on an assignment outside the UK

There are special arrangements for people who worked or were detained without pay in Iraq during the Gulf Crisis. If you think you might be affected by this, write to HM Revenue & Customs (HMRC) at:

HM Revenue & Customs
National Insurance Contributions & Employer Office
Benton Park View, Newcastle upon Tyne
NE98 1ZZ
Tel: 0300 200 3211
The State Pension age

Currently, the state pension age is 66 for men and women. There will be further increases in the state pension age to 68 for men and women. The increase in the State Pension age is being phased in and your own particular pension age depends on when you were born. The proposed changes affect people born between April 1953 and 5th April 1960. (For your own retirement age you should go to the Pensions Service Website).

Additional state pension

S2P replaced the State Earnings Related Pension (SERPS) in April 2002. SERPS was, essentially, a state second tier pension and it was compulsory to pay into this in order to supplement the basic state pension. There were drawbacks however, and many people fell through the net so S2P was introduced to allow other groups to contribute. S2P refined SERPS allowing the following to contribute:

- People caring for children under six and entitled to child benefit
- Carers looking after someone who is elderly or disabled, if they are entitled to carers allowance
- Certain people who are unable to work because of illness or disability, if they are entitled to long-term incapacity benefit or severe disablement allowance and they have been in the workforce for at least one-tenth of their working life
- Self-employed people are excluded from S2P as are employees earning less than the lower earnings limit. Married women and widows paying class 1 contributions at the reduced rate do not build up additional state pension. S2P is an earnings related scheme. This means that people on high earnings build up more pension than those on lower earnings. However, people earning at least the lower earnings limit are treated as if they have earnings at that level and so build up more pension than they otherwise would.

Contracting out

A person does not build up state additional pension during periods when they are contracted out. Contracting out means that a person has opted to join an occupational scheme or a personal pensions scheme or stakeholder pension. While contacted out, a person will pay lower National Insurance Contributions on part of earnings or some of the contributions paid by an employee and employer are 'rebated' and paid into the occupational pension scheme or other pension scheme.

Increasing your state pension

There are a number of ways in which you can increase your State Pension, particularly if you have been presented with a pension forecast which shows lack of contributions and a diminished state pension. You can fill gaps in your pension contributions or you can defer your state pension. HM Revenue and Customs have a help line on 0300 200 3300 to check your record and to receive advice on whether you have gaps and how to fill them.

Filling gaps in your record

If you wish to plug gaps in your contributions, normally you can go back 6 years to fill gaps in your record. However, if you will reached State Pension Age before April 5th 2015, special rules let you fill any gaps up to six years in total going back as far as 6th April 1975. You can make class 3 contributions to fill the gap, each contribution costs £15.30 so a full years worth costs 52 times £15.30 = £795.60). Making class three contributions can't increase your additional state pension. However Class 3 contributions do count towards the state bereavement benefits that your wife, husband or civil partner could claim if you were to die.

Deferring your state pension

Another way to boost your state pension is to delay its commencement. You can put off drawing your pension for as long as you like, there is no time limit. You must defer your whole pension, including any additional or graduated pensions and you earn an addition to the lump sum or a bigger cash sum.

In the past, if you put off drawing your own pension and your wife was getting a pension based on your NI record, her pension would also have to be deferred and she would have to agree to this. From 6th April 2010 onwards, husbands and civil partners as well as wives may be able to claim a pension based on their partners record. But a change to the rules now means that, if you defer your pension and your wife, husband or civil partner claims on your record, they no longer have to defer their pension as well. If your pension has already started to be paid, you can decide to stop payments in order to earn extra pension or lump sum. But you can only defer your pension once. You can earn an increase in the pension when it does start of 1% for every five weeks you put off the pension. This is equivalent to an increase of 10.4% for each whole year.

Alternatively, if you put off claiming your pension for at least a whole year, you can earn a one-off lump sum instead of extra pension. The lump sum is taxable but only at the top rate you were paying before getting the lump sum. Whatever the size of the sum it does not mean that you move tax brackets. The Pension Service, which is part of the Department of Work and Pensions publishes a detailed guide to deferring your State pension.

Go to www. gov.uk-contact-pension-service.

Women and Pensions

It is a general rule that women pensioners tend to have less income than their male counterparts. Therefore, when building a retirement plan, women need to consider what steps they and their partners can take to make their financial future more secure.

Particular issues for women

These days, the rules of any particular pension scheme-whether state or private, do not discriminate between men and women. Whether male or female you pay the same to access the same level of benefits. However, this does not always mean that women end up with the same level of pension as men. This is because of the general working and lifestyle differences between men and women, for example women are more likely to take breaks from work and take part time work so they can look after family. As a result, women are more likely to pay less into a pension fund than men.

Historically, the (idealised) role of women as carers was built into the UK pensions system. Not least the state pension system. It was assumed that women would marry before having children and rely on their husbands to provide for them financially right through to retirement. As a result, women who have already retired typically have much lower incomes than men. Changes to the state scheme for people reaching state pension age from 6th April 2010 onwards, mean that most women will, in future, retire with similar state pensions as men. However if you are an unmarried women living with a partner you should be aware of the following:

The state scheme recognises wives, husbands and civil partners but not unmarried partners. This means that if your unmarried partner dies before you, you would not be eligible for the state benefits that provide support for bereaved dependants.

Occupational schemes and personal pensions typically pay survivor benefits to a bereaved partner, whether married or not. However many schemes-especially in the public sector-have recognised unmarried partners only recently and, as a result, the survivor pension for an unmarried partner may be very low.

The legal system recognises that wives, husbands and civil partners may have a claim on retirement savings built up by the other party in the event of divorce, but these will be considered along with all the other assets to be split between you and you may end up with a much lower retirement income than you had been expecting.

The legal system does not give similar rights to unmarried partners who split up. If your unmarried partner was building up pension savings for you both, he or she can walk away with all those savings and you have no legal claim on them.

Effects of changes to the state pension from 2016 on women

As we have discussed, from April 2021, the new "flat rate " state pension will typically be £179.60 a week, but only for those who have paid national insurance contributions (NIC's) for 35 years. Many women will not qualify, having taken career breaks to care for children.

If there are gaps in your entitlement then consider buying some added years of state pension which you can do in the run-up to retirement. The state pension purchase scheme is far more generous than any private pension, provided you live more than a few years in retirement. Be careful, though, that you're not going to be buying years that you'd actually make up through work between now and retirement, otherwise you could end up giving the government money for something you'd have got anyway. Voluntary NIC's cost £3.05 a week for Class 2 and £15.40 a week for Class 3 and you can normally fill gaps from the past six years. If you are due to retire after April 2016, check to see how much you will receive at gov.uk/future-pension-centre.

Have you told the government you are a carer?

The good news is that full-time unpaid carers will be entitled to the same pension as those who have worked in a paid full-time job from 2016. However, thousands of women who do not claim child benefit or carers' allowance could miss out.

These benefits signal to the Department for Work and Pensions (DWP) that an individual qualifies for NIC's. Since households earning above £50,000 are no longer eligible to claim full child benefit, and those earning over £60,000 will receive no child benefit at all, many stay-at home mums may go under the radar. Similarly if women are caring for a family member but not claiming carer's allowance their unpaid work will go unrecognised. If you are a carer but don't claim any benefits pro-actively contact the DWP to report your situation.

If your household income is over £50,000 but under £60,000 you should still register for child benefit in order to receive NIC's.

The over 80 pension

This is a non-contributory pension for people aged 80 or over with little or no state pension. If you are 80 or over, not getting or getting a reduced state pension because you have not paid enough National Insurance contributions (NI) and are currently living in England, Scotland or Wales and have been doing so for a total of 10 years or more in any continuous period of 20 years before or after your 80th birthday, you could claim the over 80 pension. The maximum amount of the over 80 state pension that you can get is currently £82.45 per week (2021/22).

Occupational pensions

Briefly, occupational pension schemes are a very important source of income. With Occupational pension schemes the contract is between the company and the pension provider. With Group Personal Pension Schemes, which we will also be discussing later, although the employer chooses the company the contract is between the employee and the pension company.

Occupational pension Schemes are one of the best ways to pay into a pension scheme as the employer has to contribute a significant amount to the pot. Over the years the amounts paid into occupational pension schemes has increased significantly. Although there have been a number of incidences of occupational schemes being wound up this is relatively small and they remain a key source of retirement income.

From October 2012, it has been compulsory for employers to provide an occupational pension scheme, Auto Enrolment. For the first time, employers are obliged to:

- enrol most of their workforce into a pension scheme; and
- make employer pension contributions

Stakeholder schemes

Stakeholder pension schemes are designed for those people who do not have an employer, or had an employer who did not have an occupational scheme. They therefore cannot pay into an occupational scheme. If an employer did not offer an occupational scheme (many small employers were exempt) they had to arrange access to a stakeholder scheme. Employees did not have to join an occupational scheme offered by employers, instead they could join a stakeholder scheme. Likewise, self-employed people can also join a stakeholder scheme.

Stakeholder schemes have a contribution limit-this being currently £3,600 per year. Anyone who is not earning can also pay into a scheme, up to the limit above. You pay money to a pension provider (eg an insurance company, bank or building society) who invests it (eg in shares).These are a type of personal pension but they have to meet some minimum standards set by the government. These include:

- management charges can't be more than 1.5% of the fund's value for the first 10 years and 1% after that
- you must be able to start and stop payments when you want or switch providers without being charged
- they have to meet certain security standards, eg have independent trustees and auditors.

How much can be invested in a stakeholder pension?

There is no limit to the amount that can be invested in a stakeholder pension scheme. However, tax relief can only be obtained on contributions up to a maximum annual contribution limit (known as an individual's 'annual allowance'). For the tax year 2020/21, this is set at the lower of 100% of an individual's UK earnings or £40,000 per annum. Carry forward of unused allowances may be permitted in some circumstances. It is possible to contribute up to £4,000 per year (including tax relief) into a stakeholder pension scheme even if a person is not earning. A member of an occupational pension scheme may also contribute to a stakeholder pension scheme. You can start making payments into a stakeholder pension from £20 per month. You can pay weekly or monthly. If you don't want to make regular payments you can pay lump sums any time you want.

The rules for stakeholder pensions changed on 1 October 2012. If you're starting a new job now or returning to one, your employer doesn't have to offer you access to a stakeholder pension scheme. They now have to offer entry through automatic enrolment. If you're in a stakeholder pension scheme that was arranged by your employer before 1 October 2012, they must continue to take and pay contributions from your wages. This arrangement is in place until:

- you ask them to stop
- you stop paying contributions at regular intervals
- you leave your job
- If you leave your job or change to another personal pension, the money they have paid in stays in your pension pot unless you have it transferred to a different pension provider.

Other ways to save for retirement

The government offers certain tax advantages to encourage pension saving. However, the most advantageous savings plan is the Individual Savings Account (ISA) discussed previously. In addition, you might have regular savings accounts, your home or a second home. All of these possibilities must be factored in when arriving at an adequate retirement income.

****

Chapter 3

Private Pension Savings

The lifetime allowance

There is a single lifetime limit on the amount of savings that a person can build up through various pension schemes and plans that are subject to tax relief. (This excludes the state pension). The lifetime allowance is £1,073,100m from April 2021.

The lifetime allowance applies to savings in all types of pension schemes including occupational pensions and stakeholder schemes. There are, broadly, two types of scheme or plan:

- Defined contribution-with these types of schemes money goes in and is invested with the fund used to buy a pension. Basically, if the fund at retirement is £200,000 then £200,000 lifetime allowance has been used up
- Defined benefit-in this type of scheme, a person is promised a pension of a certain amount usually worked out on the basis of salary before retirement and the length of time that you have been in the scheme. The equation for working out lifetime benefit in this type of scheme is a little more complicated. The pension is first converted into a notional sum (the amount of money it is reckoned is needed to buy a pension of that size). The government sets out a factor that it says will be needed to make the conversion which it has said is 20. If the pension is £20,000 then this is calculated as £20,000

times £20,000 which is £400,000. Therefore £400,000 will be used up from the lifetime allowance.

Protecting the Lifetime Allowance

The standard lifetime allowance is £1,073,100 on 6 April 2021. But you may be able to protect your pension savings from the annual reductions. These reductions can be complicated and to get full details you should go to:

https://www.gov.uk/guidance/pension-schemes-protect-your-lifetime-allowance

The annual allowance

The annual allowance (amount that an individual can contribute to a pension) is £40,000 (April 2021). This is the amount that pension savings may increase each year whether through contributions paid in or to promised benefits. In addition, you can carry forward unused allowances from three years previously the annual allowance will not start in the year a person starts their pension or die. This gives a person scope to make large last-minute additions to their fund. If at retirement the value of a pension exceeds the lifetime allowance there will be an income tax charge of 55% on the excess if it is taken as a lump sum, or 25% if it is left in the scheme to be taken as a pension, which is taxable as income. If the increase in the value of savings in any year exceeds the annual allowance, the excess is taxed at 40%.

Limits to benefits and contributions

The present benefit and contribution limits have been scrapped. The only remaining restrictions are:

- Contributions-the maximum that can be paid in each year is either the amount equal to taxable earnings or £3,600 whichever is the greater
- Tax free lump sum-at retirement a person can take up to one quarter of the value of the total pension fund as a tax free lump sum

Taking a pension

Savings do not have to be converted into pension in one go. This can be staggered and pension income can be increased as a person winds down from work.

For each tranche of pension started before 75, there is a range of choices. This will depend on the rules of each individual scheme. A person can:

- Have a pension paid direct from an occupational pension scheme
- Use a pension fund to purchase an annuity to provide a pension for the rest of life
- Use part of the pension to buy a limited period annuity lasting just five years leaving the rest invested
- Opt for income drawdown which allows taking of a pension whilst leaving the rest invested. The tax-free lump sum could be taken and the rest left invested. The maximum income will be 120% of a standard annuity rate published by the Financial Conduct Authority. On death the remaining pension fund can be used to provide pensions for dependants or paid to survivors as a lump sum, taxed at 35%.

From 6 April 2015, where the member dies before the age of 75, spouses or other beneficiaries who inherit joint life or guaranteed term annuities will no longer be taxed on the income. This aligns their treatment with dependant drawdown pensions.

It was also confirmed that drawdown pensions paid to spouses, or other dependants or nominees, would be tax-free where the member died before reaching the age of 75 and the pension first comes into payment on or after 6 April 2015. The fund can also be passed on tax-free as a lump sum, rather than potentially being subject to a 55% charge.

Not all dependant pensions will benefit from the tax exemption, however. Where the member dies before the age of 75 with either uncrystallised funds or a drawdown fund, if the beneficiary chooses to buy an annuity with the fund rather than go into drawdown, this will remain fully taxable. Similarly, there is no provision for making inherited scheme pensions (eg widow's pensions from final salary schemes) tax-free. Where the member dies after reaching the age of 75, all dependant pensions remain taxable, as they are under the current rules. Dependants who are already in receipt of annuities before 6 April 2015 will remain taxed on them in the same way as dependant drawdown pensions.

When a person reaches 75 years of age, they must opt for one of the following choices:

- Have a pension paid direct from an occupational scheme
- Use the pension fund to buy an annuity to provide a pension for the rest of life or
- Opt for an Alternatively Secured Pension or ASP. This is pension draw down but with the maximum income

limited to 90% of the annuity rate for a 75 year old. On death, the remaining fund can be used to provide dependants pensions or, if there are no dependants, left to a charity or absorbed into the scheme to help other people's pensions. The person(s) whose pensions are to be enhanced can be nominated by the person whose pension it is.

We will be discussing options for taking pensions in more depth in Chapter 15

****

Chapter 4

Personal Pension Plans

There is a wide choice of personal pension schemes on offer. One common denominator is that the schemes are now heavily regulated by both the government and the Financial Conduct Authority. Most schemes will accept either a monthly contribution or a one-off lump sum payment per annum. The majority of schemes will allow a person to increase contributions. It is important to look for a plan that will allow a person to miss payments, in case of unemployment, sickness etc, without penalty.

Investments

Plans which allow individuals to choose their own investments are called' Self-invested Personal Pensions' (SIIPS) (see below). A person will build up their own fund of personal investments from a wide range of options such as shares, gilts, property and other areas. However, unless an individual has a large sum to invest, this is unlikely to be a wise bet. Pension companies can offer their own expertise and usually have far greater knowledge than the individual.

Self-invested Personal Pensions (Sipps)

A self-invested personal pension (SIPP) is a pension 'wrapper' that holds investments until you retire and start to draw a retirement income. It is a type of personal pension and works in a similar way to a standard personal pension. The main difference is that with a SIPP, you have more flexibility with the investments you can choose.

How it works

SIPPs aren't for everyone. Get advice if you're thinking about this type of personal pension. With standard personal pension schemes, your investments are managed for you within the pooled fund you have chosen. SIPPs are a form of personal pension that give you the freedom to choose and manage your own investments. Another option is to pay an authorised investment manager to make the decisions for you.

SIPPs are designed for people who want to manage their own fund by dealing with, and switching, their investments when they want to. SIPPs can also have higher charges than other personal pensions or stakeholder pensions. For these reasons, SIPPs tend to be more suitable for large funds and for people who are experienced in investing.

What you can and can't invest in

Most SIPPs allow you to select from a range of assets, such as:
- Unit trusts.
- Investment trusts.
- Government securities.
- Insurance company funds.
- Traded endowment policies.
- Some National Savings and Investment products.
- Deposit accounts with banks and building societies.
- Commercial property (such as offices, shops or factory premises).

- Individual stocks and shares quoted on a recognised UK or overseas stock exchange.

These aren't all of the investment options that are available – different SIPP providers offer different investment options. It's unlikely that you'll be able to invest directly in residential property within a SIPP. Residential property can't be held directly in a SIPP with the tax advantages that usually accompany pension investments. But, subject to some restrictions, including on personal use, residential property can be held in a SIPP through certain types of collective investments, such as real estate investment trusts, without losing the tax advantages.

How you access money in your SIPP
New rules introduced in April 2015 mean you can access and use your pension pot in any way you wish from age 55, (however, see below-accessing your pension funds to finance your business).

There's a lot to weigh up when working out which option or combination will provide you and any dependants with a reliable and tax-efficient income throughout your retirement. Be sure to use the free, government-backed Pension Wise service to help you understand your options or get financial advice.

As mentioned you should note that in 2019, the **Money and Pensions Service** replaced Pension Wise, The Money Advice Service and the Pensions Advisory Service, which will all be under the new umbrella. For further information about the timing of this go to their website:
www.moneyandpensionsservice.org.uk

Small Self-Administered Schemes (Ssas)

A SSAS is essentially an employer sponsored pension scheme with fewer than 12 people, where at least one member is connected with another, or with a trustee or the sponsoring employer, and where some or all of the scheme assets are invested other than in insurance policies.

Every registered pension scheme is required to have a Scheme Administrator. If a Scheme Administrator is not appointed, then the Scheme trustees will normally become the Scheme Administrator by default. The Scheme Administrator must enrol online with HMRC before they can register the SSAS. Contributions to the SSAS must not be paid by either the employer or a member until the scheme has been registered with HM Revenue and Customs.

Any contributions, even if they are only paid to the Trustees' bank account, before the scheme is registered will not receive tax relief. The managing trustees must open a Scheme bank account. Contributions from the company (and the members) are paid into the bank account before they are invested at the managing trustees' discretion (subject to certain restrictions).

The structure of a Small Self-Administered Scheme could, for example, be as follows:

- Company and member payments
- Trustees' bank account
- Insurance Company investments

Self-administered part

– Commercial property eg. company premises.

– Loans to employer.

–Deposit accounts.

– Open Ended Investment Companies (OEICs).

– Stock Exchange

– e.g. equities.

– Securities, etc

– e.g. gilts.

– Trustee Investment Bond.

There are clear benefits to holding assets under a registered pension scheme. For example, no capital gains tax liability arises when scheme assets are sold. On the other hand, when personally-held assets are sold this can trigger a Capital Gains Tax liability.

A SSAS:

- Gives the managing trustees wide investment powers.
- Is a possible source of loan capital to the company for business expansion purposes, which may help minimise reliance on a third party (eg. bank).
- May be able to buy the company's premises – the SSAS managing trustees act as the landlord, meaning that the members retain control.
- Can be a possible source of equity capital for business expansion purposes which could avoid partial surrender of control to external interests.
- Is a vehicle for the managing trustees to back their investment judgement. A SSAS generally appeals to controlling directors who want
- To retain control over their pension benefits.
- To use the self-investment facility to help the company's development.
- A greater say in the way pension payments are invested

Releasing funds to finance business

One of the important points here is that, if the scheme is a small self-administered scheme it can be accessed to provide funds for a business, even if you are under the age of 55. This is known as 'pension-led funding'. Both SIIP's and SSAS's serve as an appropriate vehicle for this.

To effect pension-led funding you set up a sale and leaseback type arrangement whereby your pension buys assets from your business or loans money to your business secured against your retirement funds. However, it should be noted that there are advantages and disadvantages of doing this so you would need to talk the matter through with a pension provider with knowledge of this area. Scottish Widows is one such provider. There are many more. A reputable financial advisor will be able to point you in the right direction.

Fees and other charges

Those who invest your money on your behalf don't work for nothing. Fees are charged. The rate of interest offered will reflect the ultimate charge and there will probably be an administration fee too. Some plans have very complicated charging structures and it is very important that these are understood before decisions are made.

Other benefits from a personal pension

A personal pension scheme does not automatically offer a package of benefits in addition to the actual pension. Any additional benefits have to be paid for. The range of extra benefits includes lump sum life cover for dependants if death occurs before retirement, a pension for widow or widower or other partner, a waiver of contributions if there is an inability to work and a pension paid early if sickness or disability prevents working until retirement age.

A contracted out personal pension must allow for a widow's or widower's pension to be payable if the widow or widower is over 45 years of age, or is younger than 45 but qualifies for child benefit. The pension would be whatever amount can be bought by the fund built up through investing the contracting-out rebates. The widow or widower has an open market option, which gives him or her a right to shop around for a different pension provider rather than remain with the existing provider.

The pension could cease if the widow or widower remarries while under the state pension age, or ceases to be eligible for child benefit whilst still under 45. This depends on the terms of the contract at the time of death.

A contracted out widow's or widower's pension built up before 6th April 1997 must be increased each year in line with inflation, up to a maximum of 3% a year. For post April 1997 pensions this must be up to 5% per year and after 6th April 2005, pensions taken out don't have to increase at all.

With the exception of contracted out plans, a person must choose at the time of taking out the plan which death benefits to have as part of the scheme. Broadly, they should be in line with the benefits mentioned above.

Retirement due to ill-health

If a person has to retire due to ill-health, a pension can be taken from a personal plan at any age. However, a person's inability to work must be clearly demonstrated and backed up with a professional opinion.

Taking a pension early will result in a reduced pension because what is in the pot will be less. However, there are ways of mitigating this, one way to ensure that a waiver of premiums in the event of sickness is included in the pension. In this way the plan will continue to grow even though a person is ill. Another way is to take out permanent disability insurance. This insurance will guarantee that the pension that you will get when you cannot work will at least be a minimum amount.

The Pension Protection Fund

Members of defined benefit occupational pension schemes are protected through the PPF, which will pay regular compensation, based on your pension amount, if the company becomes insolvent and the pension scheme doesn't have enough money to pay your pension. The PPF applies to most defined benefit schemes where the employer became insolvent after 6th April 2005. You should check with the PPF about levels of compensation.

The Financial Assistance Scheme

If you are an individual scheme member and have lost out on your pension as a result of your scheme winding up after 1st January 1997 and the introduction of PPF, you may be able to get financial help from the FAS, which is administered by the Pension Protection Fund, if:

- your defined benefit scheme was under funded and
- your employer is insolvent, no longer exists or has entered into a valid compromise agreement with the trustees of the pension fund to avoid insolvency; or
- in some circumstances, your final salary scheme was wound up because it could not pay members benefits even if the employer continues trading.

45

In the case of fraud or theft

If the shortfall in your company pension scheme was due to Fraud or theft, it may be possible to recover some of the money through the PPF who operate what is known as the Fraud Compensation Scheme.

The Pension Tracing Service

If you think that you may have an old pension but are not sure of the details, the Pension Tracing Service, part of the Pension Service, may be able to help. They can be contacted on 0800 1223 170 (general enquiries) and will give you full details of their scheme and also will tell you what they need from you in order to trace the pension. www.pensiontracingservice.com.

****

Chapter 5

Pensions and Benefits for Dependants

State pensions

If you die before your spouse or civil partner has reached state pension age there may be some entitlement to state bereavement benefits if you have built up the appropriate NI contributions in the years prior to your death. The following may be available:

- Bereavement payment. This is a tax-free lump sum of £2500 (Standard rate for deaths occurring after 6th April 2017) or £3,500 higher rate.

- Widowed Parent's Allowance. This is a taxable income (£122.55 a week (2021/22) plus half of any additional state pension (S2P) you had built up. The payment continues until the youngest child ceases to be dependant or until your widow, widower or civil partner, enters a new marriage or civil partnership or starts to live with someone as if they were married or registered. Your spouse or civil partner might also be able to claim Child Tax Credit (CTC, a means tested state benefit available to households with children).

- Bereavement allowance. This is a regular taxable payment payable to spouses and civil partners over age 45 without any dependant children. The amount increases with their age. This is payable for a maximum of 52 weeks and will cease if a spouse or civil partner remarries.

Death after retirement

If you die after you and your spouse/civil partner have both reached State Pension age help is given through the State pension system. Your spouse or partner, if they do not receive a full basic pension in their own right, may be able to make up the pension to the full single person's rate, currently £179.60 per week (2021/22 new rate) by using your contribution record. In addition, they can inherit half of any additional State Pension you had built up.

To find out more about bereavement benefits contact your local jobcentre plus, if you are of working age at www.direct.gov.uk. Advice on a full range of bereavement benefits for those who are retired can also be obtained here.

Occupational and personal schemes

Occupational and personal schemes may also offer pensions and lump sum pay-outs for your survivors when you die. Schemes can pay pensions to your dependants (but not anyone who was not dependant or co-dependant on you) whether you die before or after you started your pension. This means your husband, wife, civil partner, children under the age of 23 or, if older, dependant on you because of physical or mental impairment.

Also, anyone else financially dependant on you can benefit. Under the tax rules, all the dependants pensions added together must not come to more than the retirement pension you would have been entitled to, but otherwise there is no limit on the amount of any one pension, although individual scheme rules may set some limits.

Dependant's pensions from occupational salary-related schemes

Subject to tax rules governing such schemes, a scheme can set its own rules about how much pension it will provide for dependants. Typically, a scheme will provide a pension for a widow, widower, civil partner or unmarried partner on:

- death before you have started your pension
- death after you have started your pension.
- This will typically be half or two thirds of the pension that you were entitled to at the time of your death. The pension must be increased in line with inflation. If you have been contracted out through a salary related pension scheme before April 1977, the scheme must pay a guaranteed minimum pension (GMP) to the person entitled equal to half the GMP's you had built up.

Lump sum death benefits

The options available to your beneficiaries after you die will depend on how you choose to take your pension and at what age you die. In the event of your death whilst in drawdown your beneficiaries will have the following options under the current rules:

- **Take the pension as a lump sum** Any beneficiary can inherit some or all of your remaining fund. They can do what they like with it. This payment will be tax free if you die before reaching age 75, or taxed at the beneficiary's marginal rate of income tax if after.
- **Continue with drawdown** A dependant or nominated beneficiary can continue to receive your fund as drawdown. Income from which will be tax free if you die

49

before reaching age 75, or taxed at the beneficiary's marginal rate of income tax if after.

- **Convert the drawdown fund to a lifetime annuity**
  A dependant or nominated beneficiary can use your remaining drawdown fund to purchase a lifetime annuity. The income will be tax free if you die before reaching age 75, or taxed at the beneficiary's marginal rate of income tax if after.

Pensions are typically held in trust outside your estate and so in most cases are free of inheritance tax (IHT). Death benefits set up more than two years after death may lose their tax-free status. If you make a pension contribution or reduce the income you are drawing from your drawdown plan while in ill health or within two years of death the funds may still be liable to IHT. Tax charges may also apply if you exceed the lifetime allowance and die before age 75.

This information is based on 6 April 2021 pension rules and is subject to change. Tax rules & benefits can change and their value will depend on your personal circumstances.

****

Chapter 6

Pensions-Options for Retirement and Tax Implications

___

Retirement options and taxation of pensions

As you will know by now, changes introduced from April 2015 give you freedom over how you can access your pension savings if you're 55 or over and have a pension based on how much has been paid into your pot (such as a defined contribution, money purchase or cash balance scheme).

Options for using your pension pot

Depending on your age and personal circumstances some or all of the options outlined below could be suitable for you. Your main options are:

1. Keep your pension savings where they are and take them later on in life.
2. Use your pension pot to get a guaranteed income for life – called a Lifetime annuity. The income is taxable, but you can choose to take up to 25% of your pot as a one-off tax-free lump sum at the outset.
3. Use your pension pot to provide a Flexible retirement income, take 25% of your pension pot (or 25% of the amount you allocate for this option) as a tax-free lump sum, then use the rest to provide a regular taxable income.

4. Take a number of lump sums – the first 25% of each cash withdrawal from your pot will be tax-free. The rest will be taxed.

5. Take your pension pot in one go – the first 25% will be tax-free and the rest is taxable.

6. Mix your options – choose any combination of the above, using different parts of your pot or separate pots.

We will now look at each of these six options, and the implications, in turn.

1. Keep your pension savings where they are

With this option, your pot continues to grow tax-free until you need it – potentially providing more income once you start taking money out. You (and your employer) can continue making contributions however there are restrictions on how much you can save each year and over a lifetime and still receive tax relief.

In most cases you can get tax relief on pension contributions, including any employer contributions, on the lower of 100% of your earnings or up to £40,000 each year (2021-22 tax year) until age 75. However, if you are a high earner the limit on how much tax-free money you can build up in your pension in any one year depends on your 'adjusted income'. If you don't pay Income Tax, you can still get tax relief on up to £3,600 of pension savings each year until age 75.

However, you will need to check with your pension scheme or provider whether there are any restrictions or charges for changing your retirement date, and the process and deadline for telling them. You need to know whether there are any costs for leaving your pot where it is – some providers charge an administration fee for continuing to manage your pension. Check that you won't lose any valuable income guarantees – for example, a guaranteed annuity rate – if you delay your retirement date.

One other important point is that the money you have saved into your pension pot could continue to grow, but it could also go down in value, as with any investment. Remember to review where your pot is invested as you get closer to the time you want to retire and arrange to move it to less risky funds if necessary.

If you want your pot to remain invested after the age of 75, you'll need to check that your pension scheme or provider will allow this. If not, you may need to transfer to another scheme or provider who will. Not all pension schemes and providers will allow you to delay. If you want to delay but don't have this option, shop around before moving your pension.

On death, any unused pension pots normally fall outside your estate for Inheritance Tax purposes and can be passed on to any nominated beneficiary. In both cases the money continues to grow tax-free while still invested.

If you die before age 75: Provided the beneficiary takes the money within two years of the provider being notified of the pension holder's death, they can take it as a tax-free lump sum or as tax-free income. If they take it later (whether as a lump sum or income) it will be added to their other income and taxed at the appropriate Income Tax rate.

If you die age 75 or over: When the money is taken out (lump sum or income) it will be added to the beneficiary's income and taxed at the appropriate Income Tax rate. However, if the beneficiary is not an individual but is, for example, a company or trust, any lump sum will be taxed at 45%.

2. Use your pension pot to get a guaranteed income for life

A guaranteed income for life – known as a lifetime annuity – provides you with a guarantee that the money will last as long as you live. Guaranteed lifetime income products include: basic lifetime annuities; Investment-linked annuities.

The options

You can choose to take up to 25% (a quarter) of your pot as a one-off tax-free lump sum at the outset. You use the rest to buy a guaranteed lifetime income – a lifetime annuity – from your provider or another insurance company. You must buy within six months of taking your tax-free lump sum. As a rule of thumb, the older you are when you take out a guaranteed lifetime income product, the higher the income you'll get. You can choose to receive your income monthly, quarterly, half-yearly or yearly, depending on the scheme or provider. This type of income is taxable.

Basic lifetime annuities

Basic lifetime annuities offer a range of income options designed to match different personal circumstances. You need to decide whether you want:

- one that provides a guaranteed income for you only and stops when you die –a single life annuity, or one that also provides an income for life for a dependant or other nominated beneficiary after you die – a joint life annuity (normally provides a lower regular income as it's designed to pay out for longer)
- payments to continue to a nominated beneficiary for a set number of years (for example 10 years) from the time the guaranteed income starts, in case you die

unexpectedly early – called a guarantee period (can be combined with a single or joint life annuity). For example, if you opt for a guarantee period of 10 years and die after two years, the payments to a nominated beneficiary would continue for eight years.

* payments fixed at the same amount throughout your life – a level annuity, or payments to be lower than a level annuity to start with but rise over time by set amounts – an escalating annuity – or in line with inflation – an inflation-linked annuity.

* value protection – less commonly used and likely to reduce the amount of income you receive, but designed to pay your nominated beneficiary the value of the pot used to buy the guaranteed lifetime income less income already paid out when you die.

Investment-linked annuities

If you're willing to take more risk in return for a potentially higher income, you could opt for an income that is investment-linked (known as an investment-linked annuity). The income you receive rises and falls in line with the value of investments that you choose when you purchase your product. So while it could pay more over the longer term than a basic annuity, your income could also fall.

Many investment-linked annuities guarantee a minimum income if the fund's performance is weak. With investment-linked annuities you can also have a dependant's pension, guarantee periods, value protection and higher rates if you have a short life expectancy due to poor health or lifestyle. Some investment-linked annuities allow you to change your investment options or allow you to take lower payments later.

Although you can't change your guaranteed income back into a pension pot, the government has announced changes which to come into force in early 2017, that may allow you to sell your product for a cash lump sum on which you may have to pay Income Tax. How much tax you pay would depend on the value of your product, and your overall income in that year.

Think carefully about whether you need to provide an income for your partner or another dependant on your death. Consider whether you should take a product which provides an increasing income. Inflation (the general rise in price of goods and services over time) can significantly reduce your standard of living over time. Investment-linked annuities offer the chance of a higher income – but only by taking extra risk. Your income could reduce if the fund doesn't perform as expected. If you're considering this option look at what your provider can offer then get financial advice.

If you buy guaranteed income with money from a pension pot you've already used for another income option (e.g. to provide a flexible retirement income) you can't take a further tax-free lump sum – even if you chose not to take a tax-free lump sum with the other option.

Not all pension schemes and providers offer guaranteed lifetime income products. Some may only offer one type, or offer to buy one on your behalf. Whatever the case, shop around before deciding who to go with – you're likely to get a better income than sticking with your current provider.

Tax

You will have to pay tax on the income you receive, in the same way you pay tax on your salary. How much you pay depends on your total income and the Income Tax rate that applies to you. Your provider will take tax off your income before you receive it

Because they won't know your overall income they will use an emergency tax code to start with. This means you may pay too much tax initially and have to claim the money back – or you may owe more tax if you have other sources of income. If the value of all of your pension savings is above £1,073,100 (2021-222 tax year) and these savings haven't already been assessed against the Lifetime allowance, further tax charges may apply when you access your pension pot.

Tax relief on future pension savings

After buying a guaranteed income product you can in most cases continue to get tax relief on pension savings of up to the Annual allowance of £40,000 (2021-22). However, if you buy a lifetime annuity which could decrease such as an investment-linked annuity, the maximum future defined contribution pension savings that can be made in a year that qualifies for tax relief is limited to the lower of £10,000 (the Money purchase annual allowance) or 100% of your earnings. If you want to carry on saving into a pension this option may not be suitable.

On death, if you have a single life guaranteed income product and no other features, your pension stops when you die. Otherwise, the tax rules vary depending on your age as shown below.

If you die before age 75: Income from a joint guaranteed income product will be paid to your dependant or other nominated beneficiary tax-free for the rest of their life. If you die within a guarantee period the remaining payments will pass tax-free to your nominated beneficiary then stop when the guarantee period ends. Any lump sum payment due from a value protected guaranteed lifetime income product will be paid tax-free. It will also normally fall outside your estate for Inheritance Tax purposes.

If you die age 75 or over: Income from a joint guaranteed income product or a continuing guarantee period will be added to the beneficiary's overall income and taxed at the appropriate Income Tax rate. Joint payments will stop when your dependant or other beneficiary dies and any guarantee period payments stop when the guarantee period ends. Any lump sum due from a value protected guaranteed income product will be added to the beneficiary's overall income and taxed at the appropriate Income Tax rate. Lump sums due from a value protected guaranteed income product normally fall outside your estate for Inheritance Tax purpose.

3. Use your pension pot to provide a flexible retirement income

You can move all or some of your pension pot into an investment specifically designed to provide an income for your retirement . The income isn't guaranteed but you have flexibility to make changes. This is sometimes called 'Flexi-access drawdown'.

You can choose to take up to 25% (a quarter) of your pension pot as a tax-free lump sum. You then move the rest within six months into one or more funds (or other assets) that allow you to take income at times to suit you – e.g. monthly, quarterly, yearly or irregular withdrawals. Most people use it to take a regular income. If you don't move the rest of your money within the six months, you'll be charged tax (normally 55% of the un-transferred fund value). Once you've taken your tax-free lump sum, you can start taking the income right away, or wait until a later date. The income is taxable.

Unlike with a guaranteed income for life (a lifetime annuity), the retirement income you receive from a flexible retirement income product is not guaranteed to last as long as you live, so you should think carefully about how much you withdraw.

Deciding how much income you can afford to take needs careful planning – it depends on how much money you put in from your pension pot, the performance of the funds, what other sources of income you have, and whether you want to provide for a dependant or someone else after you die. It also depends on how long you will live. Your retirement income could fall or even run out if you take too much too soon and start eating into the money you originally invested to produce the income – especially if stock markets fall. Investment choice is key – you will need to review where your money is invested regularly to ensure it continues to meet your long-term retirement income needs. Investments can fall as well as rise – you'll need to know how you'll cope if your income suddenly drops.

Not all pension schemes and providers offer flexible retirement income products. If yours doesn't, you can transfer your pension pot to another provider who does but again there may be a fee to do so. Different providers will offer different features and charging structures on their products – and the choice is likely to increase.

You pay tax on the income withdrawals (outside the tax-free cash allowance). How much tax you pay depends on your total income and the Income Tax rate that applies to you. Your provider will take tax off your income payments in advance. Because they won't know your overall income they will use an emergency tax code to start with which means you may initially pay too much tax – and have to claim the money back – or you may owe more tax if you have other sources of income. If you have other income, you'll need to plan carefully how much flexible retirement income to take, to avoid pushing yourself into a higher tax bracket.

Tax relief on future pension savings

Once you have taken any money from your flexible retirement income product, the maximum future defined contribution pension savings that can be made in a year that qualifies for tax relief is limited to the lower of £4,000 (the Money purchase annual allowance – down from the usual £40,000 Annual allowance in 2021-22) or 100% of your earnings. If you want to carry on building up your pension pot, this may influence when you start taking your flexible retirement income. The tax relief you get for future pension savings is not affected if you take the tax-free lump sum but no income. On death, any remaining flexible retirement income funds when you die normally fall outside your estate for Inheritance Tax purposes.

If you die before age 75: Anything remaining in your fund passed to a nominated beneficiary within two years of notifying the provider of the pension holder's death will be tax-free whether they take it as a lump sum or as income. If it is over two years any money paid will be added to the beneficiary's income and taxed at their appropriate rate.

If you die age 75 or above: Anything remaining in your fund that you pass on – either as a lump sum or income – will be taxed at the beneficiary's appropriate Income Tax rate.

4. Take your pension pot as a number of lump sums

You can leave your money in your pension pot and take lump sums from it when you need it, until your money runs out or you choose another option.

You take cash from your pension pot as and when you need it and leave the rest invested where it can continue to grow tax-free. For each cash withdrawal the first 25% (quarter) will be tax-free and the rest is taxable. There may be charges each time you make a cash withdrawal and/or limits on how many withdrawals you can make each year. Unlike with the flexible retirement income option your pot isn't re-invested into new funds specifically chosen to pay you a regular income.

This option won't provide a regular income for you, or for any dependant after you die. Your pension pot reduces with each cash withdrawal. The earlier you start taking money out the greater the risk that your money could run out – or what's left won't grow sufficiently to generate the income you need to last you into old age.

Remember, as we saw in chapter 2, the buying power of cash reduces because of rising prices over time (inflation) – using cash sums to fund your long-term retirement isn't advisable. If you plan to use cash withdrawals to make a one-off purchase or to pay down debts, you must also be sure that you have enough left to live on for the rest of your life.

In addition, it is worth noting that this option won't provide a regular retirement income for you or for any dependants after you die.

Not all pension providers or schemes offer the ability to withdraw your pension pot as a number of lump sums. Shop around if you want this option but can't get it with your current provider, as charges and restrictions will vary. You may not be able to use this option if you have primary protection or enhanced protection, and protected rights to a tax-free lump sum of more than £375,000 (protections that relate to the Lifetime Allowance).

Tax

Three-quarters (75%) of each cash withdrawal counts as taxable income. This could increase your tax rate when added to your other income. How much tax you pay depends on your total income and the Income Tax rate that applies to you. Your pension scheme or provider will pay the cash and take off tax in advance. Because they won't know your overall income they will use an emergency tax code to start with. This means you may pay too much tax and have to claim the money back – or you may owe more tax if you have other sources of income. If the value of all of your pension savings is above £1,073,100 and these savings haven't already been assessed against the Lifetime allowance (2021-22 tax year), further tax charges may apply when you access your pension pot. Once you reach age 75, if you have less remaining Lifetime allowance available than the amount you want to withdraw, the amount you will get tax-free will be limited to 25% (a quarter) of your remaining Lifetime allowance, rather than 25% of the amount you are taking out.

Tax relief on future pension savings

Once you have taken a lump sum, the maximum future defined contribution pension savings that can be made in a year that qualifies for tax relief is limited to the lower of £4,000 (the Money purchase annual allowance – down from the £40,000 Annual allowance for most people in 2019-20) or 100% of your earnings. If you want to carry on saving into a pension, this option may not be suitable.

On death any untouched part of your pension pot normally falls outside your estate for Inheritance Tax purposes.

If you die before age 75: Any untouched part of your pension pot will pass tax-free to your nominated beneficiary provided the money is claimed within 2 years of notifying the provider of the pension holder's death. If it is over 2 years the money will be added to the beneficiary's other income and taxed at the appropriate rate.

If you die age 75 or over: Any untouched part of your pension pot that you pass on - either as a lump sum or income - will be added to the beneficiary's overall income and taxed at the appropriate Income Tax rate.

5. Take your pension pot in one go

You no longer have to convert your pension pot into an income if you don't want to. You can take out all of your pension savings in one go if you wish. Cashing in your pension pot will not give you a secure retirement income. Basically, you close your pension pot and withdraw it all as cash. The first 25% (quarter) will be tax-free and the rest will be taxable.

This option won't provide a regular income for you – or for your spouse, civil partner or other dependant after you die. Three-quarters (75%) of the amount you withdraw is taxable income, so there's a strong chance your tax rate would go up when the money is added to your other income. If you choose this option you can't change your mind – so you need to be certain that it's right for you. For many or most people it will be more tax efficient to consider one or more of the other options. If you plan to use the cash to clear debts, buy a holiday, or indulge in a big-ticket item you need to think carefully before committing to this option.

Doing so will reduce the money you will have to live on in retirement, and you could end up with a large tax bill.

In addition, you may not be able to use this option if you have primary protection or enhanced protection, and protected rights

63

to a tax-free lump sum of more than £375,000 (protections that relate to the LIfetime Allowance). It is best to talk to your scheme if you have one or more of these kinds of protection and find out what your options are. There may be charges for cashing in your whole pot. Check with your scheme or provider. Not all pension schemes and providers offer cash withdrawal – shop around then get financial advice if you still want this option after considering its risks, as charges may vary.

Tax relief on future pension savings

Once you have cashed in your pension pot, the maximum future defined contribution pension savings that can be made in a year that qualifies for tax relief is limited to the lower of £4,000 (the Money purchase annual allowance – down from the usual £40,000 Annual allowance which will apply for most people in 2021-22) or 100% of your earnings.

On death, whatever age you die, any money remaining or investments bought with cash taken out of your pension pot will count as part of your estate for Inheritance Tax. By contrast, any part of your pot that was untouched would not normally be liable.

6. Mixing your options

You don't have to choose one option – you can mix and match as you like over time or over your total pension pot, whichever suits your needs. You can also keep saving into a pension if you wish, and get tax relief up to age 75. Which option or combination is right for you will depend on:

- when you stop or reduce your work
- your income objectives and attitude to risk

- your age and health
- the size of your pension pot and other savings
- any pension or other savings of your spouse or partner, if relevant
- the possible effect on your entitlement to State benefits
- whether you have financial dependants
- whether your circumstances are likely to change in the future.

Tax-free lump sums when mixing options

Note that depending on how you access money from your pension pot you may only get one chance to take your tax-free amount. This can be anything up to 25% (a quarter) of the amount you access and must be taken at that time. For example, if you use your whole pension pot to provide a flexible retirement income, you use up your rights to take a tax-free sum at the time you transfer the funds. So whether you choose to take 25% tax-free, or less – or no tax-free sum at all – you can't take a tax-free lump sum later if, for example, you decide to use part of your flexible retirement income fund to buy a guaranteed income for life (an annuity). However, if you only used part of your pot to buy a flexible retirement income and later wanted to use some or all of the remaining part of your pension pot to buy a regular income for life (a lifetime annuity), you could take up to 25% of that money as tax-free cash.

On death, the same rules apply for passing on your remaining pension as already set out for each option.

For more advice on pensions and tax go to www.pensionsadvisoryservice.org.uk

****

Chapter 7

Reaching Retirement Age

_____

We have discussed many of the issues in this section in previous chapters. Nevertheless it is worth reiterating them as when you reach retirement age you will want to know the practical issues such as how do you claim your pension.

On reaching retirement age, it will be necessary to ensure that all paperwork relating to pension contributions is in order. There are a number of rules that should be observed in order to ensure that any pension due is paid:

- keep all documents relating to pension rights
- start organising any pension due before retirement, this will ensure that any problems are overcome well before retirement

It is very important that communication is kept with all pension providers, and that they have accurate up-to-date records of a person's whereabouts. Each time addresses are changed this should be communicated to all pension providers. If it is impossible to track down an old employer from whom a pension is due, the Pension Schemes Registry can help. The Pensions Regulator is responsible for the Pension Schemes Registry. This was set up in 1990, by the government to help people trace so-called 'lost pensions'. If help is needed this can be obtained by filling in a form which can be accessed on the website of the pensions regulator www.pensionsregulator.gov.uk

How to claim state pension

A letter will be sent to all retiree's about four months before retirement date. This will come from the pension service and will detail how much pension is due. The pension is not paid automatically, it has to be claimed. This can be done by phoning the Pensions Claim Line number included with the letter, or by filling in a claim form BR1. If the person is a married man and the wife is claiming based on the husbands contributions, then form BF225 should be filled in. If the pension is to be deferred it is advisable to contact the Pensions Service in writing as soon as possible at www. pensionsadvisoryservice.org.uk. A late pension claim can be backdated up to twelve months. If a man is claiming for a pension for his wife based on his contributions this can only be backdated six-months.

How the pension is paid

Pensions are paid by the DWP pension direct to a bank account or Post Office Card Account. To find out more about the payment of pensions contact the DWP www.gov.uk/government/organisations/department-for-work-pensions.

Leaving the country

If a person goes abroad for less than six months, they can carry on receiving pension in the normal way. If the trip is for longer then the Pension Service should be contacted and one of the following arrangements can be made to pay a pension: Have it paid into a personal bank account while away; arrange for it to be paid into a Post Office Card Account; arrange for the money to be paid abroad; If a person is living outside of the UK at the time of the annual pension increase they won't qualify for the increase unless they reside in a member country of the European Union or a country with which the UK has an agreement for increasing pensions. It is very important that you check what will happen to your state pension when you move abroad. The DWP International Pension Centre can help on 0191 218 7777, or access advice through their main website www.gov.uk/international-pension-centre.

Pensions from an occupational scheme

Although different schemes have different arrangements, there are similar rules for each scheme. About three months before a person reaches normal retirement age, they should contact the scheme. Either telephone or write enclosing all the details that they will need. The following questions should be asked:

- What pension is due?
- What is the lump-sum entitlement?
- How will the pension be reduced if a lump sum is taken?
- How will the pension be paid, will there be any choices as to frequency?
- Is there a widow's or widowers pension, and if so how will it affect the retirement pension?
- Are there any pensions for other dependants in the event of death?

If a person has been making Additional Voluntary Contributions, then a detailed breakdown of these will be needed.

A pension from a personal plan

In the same way as a pension from an occupational scheme, it is necessary to get in touch with the pension provider about 3-4 months before retirement date.

The main questions that should be asked are:

- How much is the pension fund worth?
- How much pension will the plan provider offer?
- Can an increase be arranged each year and if so how much is the increase?
- What is the maximum lump sum?
- Is there a widow's or widowers or other dependants pension?
- What are the other options if any?
- Can the purchase of an annuity be deferred without affecting the drawing of an income?

Pensions can only be paid by an insurance company or a friendly society so if the pension has been with any other form of provider then it has to be switched before it can be paid.

If there are protected-rights from a contracted out pension plan, these can be, may have to be, treated quite separately from the rest of a pension. Protected rights from a personal pension cannot be paid until a person has reached 60 years of age. A person must, by law, have an open market option enabling protected rights pension to be paid by another provider, if it is desired.

New regulations for pension providers

As we have discussed, at the end of February 2015, the government introduced new regulations that pension providers must abide by. Pension providers will have to give specific risk warnings to savers looking to take advantage of the 2015 reforms. Any regulated company that sells policies that offer a retirement income will have to tell customers about the tax implications of cashing in or investing their pension once the reforms are fully enacted from April 6th 2015. Pension companies must also highlight how a savers health could affect their retirement income. The providers must also provide advice on the effect on benefits and also warn of scams.

Advice schemes for pensions

To help people with the transition, the government introduced a new advice service called Pension Wise. This is administered through The Pensions Advisory Services (TPAS) and the Citizens Advice Bureau. This was rolled out in March and April 2015 (as stated currently being merged into the Money and Pensions Service). Pensioners with defined contribution pension savings-either a workplace money purchase plan or a personal pension plan-will be able to access the scheme. They should be 55 or over or near retirement and can register through the Pension Wise website www.pensionwise.gov.uk.

Customers will have to book an appointment to receive either phone based advice or one to one advice and the sessions will last up to 45 minutes. Guidance will include life expectancy, long term care needs, various pension products from annuities to drawdown and a tax calculator. The guidance is not the same as regulated financial advice, such as how to invest your money but is general guidance.

Beware of Scams

As we all know, there are scammers in every walk of life (we will be discussing scams further on in chapter 19). This is how they make their living, usually having failed in legitimate enterprise. There have been warnings of increased scamming activity since the chancellor first announced the changes. Basically, scammers cold call people, promising to unlock pensions, luring people with promises of sky high returns on a number of ludicrous schemes, such as investment in property etc. In reality they are running off with your cash, leaving you with a sky high tax bill and no money.

The fundamental rule is: **avoid any cold callers** and those who promise anything at all. Avoid looking for free advice on the internet. **It is all bogus**. Manage your money yourself, after taking advice and guidance from the government scheme or through a financial advisor who is regulated by the Financial Conduct Authority. Always make sure that you are aware of the level of fees charged by financial advisors, as sometimes they can be quite high. Don't feel that you have to rush in if you are over 55. Take your time and consider the options carefully.

The Pensions Dashboard

At the time of writing (2021) the government is still working on the proposed pensions dashboard. This will be an extremely useful site when it materialises which will enable workers and retirees to see all of their pensions details, both private and state pensions, on one website. For more information concerning the pensions dashboard and its progress go to pensionsdashboardproject.uk/saver/about-the-pensions-dashboard

Inheriting pensions on death

One important factor is the question of to whom do you leave your pension on death? Are your retirement policies updated in relation to who gets your pensions or is there a danger of the pension being passed on to the wrong person, such as an ex-husband or boyfriend or someone else who you would not like to see receive the pension?

The rise in the number of divorces, remarriages and couples co-habiting, plus a general apathy towards dealing with pensions when retirement is decades away, means many people could inadvertently be handing valuable benefits to former partners.

Pension schemes typically have a form that allows members to name the person they want their benefits to go to when they die "expressions of wishes".

Make sure that all of your details are updated to ensure that any benefits go to the person you want them to go to!

****

PART 2
GENERAL FINANCIAL ISSUES

Chapter 8

Decisions Concerning Your Home

It is advisable, when reaching retirement age, to carry out an examination of the home that you live in You may decide that the home that you live in will not be suitable in the future and you may want to change, probably to something smaller or in an area where you would rather be. It could even eventually be abroad. There is also the option of moving to a care home, or housing for older people. All these options will be explored here. In addition, housing options for those with limited capital will be explored.

In many cases, those who retire and are considering selling their home will have lived in the property for many years, often raising children there. Over the years, many contacts and friendships will have formed in the community. Therefore, a number of questions need to be asked when considering selling up and moving, or giving up a rented home and moving:

- Do you still have an affinity to the area and is it likely to change in the future?
- Are you still near relatives and friends or have these patterns of friendship changed over the years and have your relatives moved on?
- Is your home expensive to run and maintain? How will this affect your finances in the future as you reach retiring age?

By releasing capital through the sale of your home and downsizing/moving area will this help your finances in the future? The sale of a larger home and the purchase of a smaller property or renting of a more age specific property can release capital which can be utilised as part of your pension plan or for liquid capital to give you a better quality of life in your retirement. If you do decide to make a move then there are also a few important points to consider:

- Will the property be easy to convert as your needs change with age?
- Is the area that you are moving to convenient in terms of amenities, doctors, hospitals etc?
- Is the area quiet in the daytime or is it noisy?
- Is the property secure?

It may well be worth doing an analysis of the good and bad points of your current home before making any decision. Of course, it may well be that, notwithstanding the good points of your current home, it is simply too large to continue to occupy, too expensive and a move is essential. When making your decision, it is well worth looking at Housing Options for Older People (HOOP). www.housingcare.org which is a self-assessment form for people wondering whether to move. The form is available from the Elderly Accommodation Council www.eac.org.uk (see useful addresses)

Moving to retirement housing

As we all know, retirement housing was hit very badly during the pandemic. However, things have stabilised and this is one option that you may well want to consider.

Retirement housing falls into several categories depending on need. It is usually available for those over 60, although there are a number of schemes which are designed for the over 55's. These schemes usually comprise of a number of flats, some with a resident warden, most with an alarm system connected to a central base which can summon help in the event of an emergency.

There are many different types of schemes. You basically get what you pay for and those with a number of services will have a corresponding service charge to match.

Many schemes will have a communal laundry and also, in some cases, a kitchen and dining room where meals can be purchased. A guest room is also usually available.

You may decide that sheltered housing (as it is usually referred to) is the ideal choice for you. The presence of a scheme manager might be reassuring and the company of others in a communal area may suit you. However, before deciding on this option, you need to weigh up the advantages and disadvantages of more sheltered housing. There will be the feeling of being 'herded' together and the loss of independence. If you feel like this you should also see whether you can receive the range of services offered in sheltered housing in your own home.

Renting retirement housing

Most retirement homes for rent are provided by local authorities and housing associations, although not all. There are also a number of schemes offered by the larger private providers although they have to manage to high standards set by local authorities. The Elderly Accommodation Counsel can offer advice.

Purchasing a retirement home

Retirement housing for sale is usually constructed by private developers although an increasing number of housing associations are also providing this type of accommodation now. Once all the properties in a scheme have been sold then the management of the scheme will be handed over to a private management company or housing association. The management organisation will be responsible for the overall management and service provision. Most retirement homes are sold on a leasehold basis with an annual ground rent (typically £250 per annum) and with a service charge that will depend on what services you are being provided. These can range from skeletal to intensive depending on your requirements.

When purchasing a retirement home it is always wise to buy off a developer who is registered with the National House Building Council (NHBC). The NHBC has a code of practice applying to all retirement homes built after 1st April 1990. If you are seriously considering buying into, or renting retirement housing there are a number of important points to consider:

- As with all housing, is the property in a convenient location and will it cater for your needs when you get older?
- What are the facilities within the scheme?
- Will the new property take your existing furniture or will you have to sell this and buy new?
- Most important, are the managing agents experienced in managing retirement housing?
- Who runs the management association, will leaseholders have a say in running it?
- How much is the service charge and what does it cover?

- What is the ground rent?
- What are the other expenses involved?
- If there is a separate sinking fund for future major repairs how do residents contribute to it?
- What are the arrangements for resale?
- Does the lease cover what will happen if your health deteriorates whilst you are in the property?
- Who owns the freehold of the property?

The above questions should be answered by the information provided in the Purchasers Information Pack which must be provided. The NHBC Code of Practice sets out what information should be in the pack.

Although many basic rights of leaseholders have been developed over the years and are enshrined in law, the lease is still paramount in terms of what services you will receive, how they are provided and what they will cost.

Invaluable advice for those living in, or intending to move into, retirement housing is provided by First Stop www.firststopcareadvice.org.uk See useful addresses. First Stop provides useful written information, prepared in conjunction with The Leasehold Advisory Service called Leasehold Retirement Housing, Your Rights and Remedies.

Options for people with limited resources
Most retirement housing is sold, as with other housing, at full market value. It follows that when you sell you get the current market value. When you sell your own property and look for retirement housing, you might find yourself in a position of not being able to buy elsewhere. This has particularly been the case in the last few years of spiralling house prices and the general

79

distortions of the British housing scene. If you are in the position of not being able to buy elsewhere after selling your home, there are a few options to consider.

Shared ownership housing

Some housing associations and, increasingly due to over-development, private developers, run schemes where you can part buy and part-rent. There are all sorts of names used to describe this model, such as homebuy: www.homebuyservice.co.uk but essentially it is what it always has been, shared ownership. In this case, you buy a percentage of the value of the property, say 25%, and then you rent the other 75%. On top of this there will be a service charge (with flats and some houses). It is not the cheapest way to obtain housing but it ensures that you get your foot on the property ladder. You should make enquiries of your local housing association which will point you in the right direction.

Lifetime lease

Some companies offer a lifetime lease, or occupancy, which means that you buy the right to live in your home for the rest of your life. The properties are sold below the market price but you will probably get very little back if you need to move again. They are also known as life interest plans.

To find out if there are any schemes in your area you should contact your local council or the Elderly Accommodation Council (address at back of this book).

Moving to rented accommodation

If you wish to move home but cannot afford to buy elsewhere, then renting privately is another option. Rented accommodation is provided in the main by local authorities, housing associations and the private sector. It is easier to rent privately than through the public sector as there is quite often a long waiting list for property and your capital may rule you out. However, tenancies in the private sector are usually insecure in that they are let out on assured shorthold tenancies which usually have a fixed duration of six months. If you wish to rent privately you should always try to go for a minimum term of twelve months. Property investors who are holding onto property for a longer term will usually be willing to do this as they are always on the lookout for a good tenant who will pay their rent.

Remember, from June 1st 2019, lettings agents and landlords are not allowed to charge fees when letting property, although there are certain fees a landlord can charge during the course of a tenancy.

Also, tenants deposits are capped at 5 weeks. For more information on this area go to www.arla.co.uk/letting-agent-fees.asp

Options for existing public sector tenants

If you are already a local authority or housing association tenant, and wish to relocate to another area, you may be able to exchange your home with another council or association tenant. This will be dependant on whether the exchange is suitable, taking into account the size of the respective properties or whether any possession orders or rent arrears exist. The council or association cannot unreasonably refuse the exchange. You will find details of exchange schemes at your local council or by making enquiries to your local housing association. The Internet also has details of several national exchange schemes.

Right to buy

If you have been a council tenant for five years or more you will usually have the right to purchase your property at a discount. The discounts are now more generous, at the time of writing. You won't usually be entitled to buy your home if you are a housing association tenant, although there are some exceptions such as stock transfers from local authorities to associations where the right to buy is preserved. In addition, the current government has promised to extend right to buy to housing association tenants. You won't, however, be able to exercise the right to buy in housing that is exclusively reserved for elderly people.

Moving to specialist housing

People who are finding it difficult to manage on their own may prefer to move to some sort of specialist housing. In addition to retirement or sheltered housing which has been outlined, there are various types of special housing to suit differing needs.

Extra care retirement housing

Some local councils and housing associations provide sheltered housing that provides extra levels of care. This housing is for people who need personal care services, such as help with dressing or bathing. This accommodation is usually provided in flats and there will normally be a shared lounge and dining rooms where meals are available. Housing in this category is usually run jointly with local authorities and people are placed there after a social services assessment. For more information on such schemes you should contact the Elderly Accommodation Council

Almshouses

Almshouses are run by charitable trusts and in turn provide accommodation for older people. Each charity will have its own rules about the types of people that they house. A few almshouses can provide extra care for vulnerable residents. Residents, as the beneficiaries of charity, do not have the same legal rights as other tenants. The individuals rights will be outlined in a 'letter of appointment' provided by the trustees or the clerk to the trustees. For more information on Almshouses, contacts the Almshouses Association, www.almshouses.org address at the back of this book.

Abbeyfield houses

Abbeyfield provides housing for people in need of sheltered accommodation. Usually this will consist of unfurnished bedsits with shared lounges, dining rooms and a shared garden. The weekly charge will include two meals a day, prepared by a resident housekeeper and also facilities for residents to prepare their own breakfasts and also snacks during the day. Typically, an Abbeyfield resident will be over 75 who is supported by a network of local volunteers. Further details can be obtained from the Abbeyfield Society address at the back of the book.

Housing for those with a disability

Many councils and associations have properties which have been specially designed for people with disabilities. This is referred to as mobility or wheelchair housing. In addition, grants are available for converting existing with disabled access. Councils and housing associations also now build what is known as lifetime homes which are designed to be adapted to peoples needs as they get older.

Living with a relative

If you are thinking of moving in with a relative, or a friend, or if you are thinking of having an older relative live with you, you should always weigh up the pros and the cons of such a move. Some of the things to consider are:

- How well will you get on with the person under the same roof?
- Is there enough space?
- Will a downstairs bedroom be needed?
- Is the housing conveniently situated?
- What are the financial arrangements?
- What are the practical arrangements, such as cooking and washing?
- What would be the implications if you or your relative needed extra care?

You should also speak to your local benefits office about the implications for benefits received when you have made the move.

Moving abroad

Many people dream of leaving the UK and moving to a warmer climate when they have retired. However, both the climate due to the pandemic and also the financial climate have changed significantly in the last few years and thorough research is necessary before contemplating such a move. Many people have moved away, particularly to places like Spain, and have returned after a few years, either disillusioned or lonely or having lost money on a property that they have purchased. The situation following BREXIT has further complicated the situation.

It is fairly easy to make enquiries about residency requirements in the various countries. The Foreign and Commonwealth office can provide information and contact details for the relevant consulates or embassies in the various countries. However, before even contemplating such a move, there are various questions that you need to address:

- Can you afford to move to another country? You have to be very clear about your financial situation in retirement. House prices abroad may seem cheap compared to the UK. However, the process of buying can be complicated and some countries, such as Spain, can be problematic, particularly now after BREXIT.
- You will need to think carefully about pension rights and health costs abroad, particularly after BREXIT.
- What about possessions? You will need specialist advice about furniture and so on, and the costs of moving.
- Can you take pets? You should always ask a vet's advice first. The Pet Travel Scheme (PETS) allows dogs and cats to re-enter the UK from certain countries without quarantine as long as they meet certain conditions. You can get further information from the Department for Environment, Food and Rural Affairs' PETS Helpline www.defra.gov.uk
- Will you want to find work? You will need professional advice about work permits in the respective countries.

Buying a property abroad

There are property magazines covering homes for sale or rent. Also, property developers are represented at retirement exhibitions. However, a word of caution, you will certainly need professional advice before embarking on a property purchase. It might be useful to buy a book on purchasing a property abroad. You will find case studies of people who have bought successfully and others who have had bad experience. For certain you will need to do your homework well. There are UK firms of solicitors who specialise in the purchase of property abroad. Addresses for such solicitors can typically be found on the Internet.

Repairs and Improvements

One of the most important elements of your home is that of its condition. When you retire or are close to retiring, this presents the ideal opportunity to assess the overall condition of your home and to draw up a condition survey (or have one drawn up) so that you can plan expenditure. It is wise to commence the work as soon as possible after retirement, or before if possible, so that you can still carry out works yourself, without resorting to using building firms. This will save money and mean that you have more control. This chapter also points the way to the various agencies that exist which will give you advice on repairs and maintenance and also funding.

Deciding what needs to be carried out

There are specialist advice agencies, called Home Improvement Agencies (sometimes called Care and Repair or Staying Put) that will give specialist advice to older and vulnerable householders and also to people living in private rented accommodation. They are small scale, not-for-profit organisations, usually managed locally by housing associations, councils or charities. They will usually offer practical help with tasks such as arranging a condition survey, getting estimates from builders (trusted builders) applying for grants or loans and also keeping an eye on the progress of work. They may charge a fee towards their assistance, which is usually included in the grant or loans that you may be in receipt of.

To find out whether there is a home improvement agency in your area, you should contact your local Age UK or the local council housing department or Foundations (the National Co-ordinating Body for Home Improvement Agencies) address at the rear of the book.

If there is no Home Improvement Agency in your area you might want to engage a surveyor to carry one out for you. As these are costly, or can be, you should always ask what the cost will be first. The Chartered Surveyor Voluntary Service exists to help people who would other wise be able to get professional advice. You need to be referred to them by a Citizens Advice Bureau first.

Finding a Builder
If there is no Home Improvement Agency in your area, you should take care, great care, when trying to find a good reliable builder. We have all heard stories of rogue builders who carry out shoddy work and charge over the odds. If you intend to employ a builder, particularly for a larger job, then you should always employ a builder backed by a proper guarantee scheme. The Federation of Master Builders (FMB) offers a MasterBond Warranty: its members must meet certain criteria and adhere to the FMB's Code of Practice. The ten-year insurance backed warranty will add 1.5% to the total cost of a job but is money well spent. Information on this scheme can be obtained from the FMB website at www.fmb.org.uk. To ensure that you get a good job done, the FMB recommends that you:

- Always ask for references and names of previous clients
- Get estimates from two or three builders
- Ask for the work to be covered by an insurance backed warranty
- Get a written specification and quotation
- Use a contract (the FMB has a plain English contract for small works)
- Agree any staged and final payments before a job
- Avoid dealing in cash

The FMB has played a leading role in the development of the government backed TrustMark scheme, which is a consumer protection initiative for the home repair and improvement sector. A wide range of traders, including plumbers and electricians, are being licensed to become TrustMark registered firms. For more information contact TrustMark address at the rear of this book.

Financial help with repairs and improvements

Sometimes, individuals find themselves in a position where they cannot afford repairs to their homes. There are, however, various forms of assistance at hand. Local authorities have general powers to provide help with repairs and also adaptations to housing. The assistance isn't always cash based, it can also be provided in the form of labour material or advice. The cash element will usually be either grants or loans. Local authorities will have published policies explaining the various forms of assistance. These can vary from time to time, as many of them are dependant on national legislation and government funding. Below are a few of the types of grants available.

Disabled facilities grant

These grants provide facilities and adaptations to help a disabled person to live as independently and in as much comfort as possible. They are means tested, i.e. dependant on income, with the exception of grants for disabled children. In its assessment, the council will take into account only your income and that of your partner or spouse. The government website www.gov.uk/disabled-facilities-grants outlines all the relevant criteria.

Social services departments provide funding for some minor adaptation works. They may also be able to help with some types of work not covered by the disabled facilities grant.

The Care and Repair England publication also provides useful information about organising and financing building works. You can get a copy by phoning 0115 950 6500 or by downloading it from the website www.careandrepair-england.org.uk.

Adapting your home

You may need to make certain adaptations to your home if you or a member of your family needs them, such as mobility aids, to make it easier to navigate the house. There are other areas that can be helpful, such as the positioning of the furniture. Occupational Therapists can give detailed advice. They can assess a person's mobility and their ability to move around and can provide appropriate advice. You should contact your local social services department and ask for an assessment of needs. You don't have to have a letter from the doctor but this can speed things up. Social services should provide some equipment free if you or a relative is assessed as needing them. All minor adaptations costing less than £1000 must be provided free of charge.

For full information about special equipment and furniture, contact Living Made Easy (formerly the Disabled Living Foundation) www.livingmadeeasy.org.uk at the address at the rear of the book.

****

Ch. 9

Raising Money from your Home

___

Equity release schemes

The main principle behind equity release schemes, which enable you to release cash from your home, is that you are offered a lump sum or an income now but you, or your estate, have to pay back a larger sum to compensate the investors (the Equity release companies). This amounts to a longer-term loan which is paid back later with rolled up interest. If you wish to raise money but do not wish to move home then these schemes could be for you.

Equity release schemes come in two basic forms: lifetime mortgages and home reversion schemes.

Lifetime mortgages

With a lifetime mortgage you borrow against the value of your home but the capital, and usually the interest are repaid only on your death or when you move out. Lifetime mortgages can be taken out jointly with your spouse or partner, in which case the loan does not have to be repaid until the second death. You can use a lifetime mortgage to raise a single large cash sum. If you want an income you can draw out a series of smaller sums or use a single lump sum to buy an investment, such as an annuity. The former is more tax efficient because the income from an annuity is usually taxable.

Types of lifetime mortgages

With the most common form of lifetime loan-a roll up loan-interest is added each month to the amount that you owe. You are charged interest not just on the amount that you originally borrowed, but to the increasing balance as interest is added. The interest can be fixed for the whole life of the loan or can be variable. When your home is eventually sold, the proceeds are used to repay the outstanding loan and what is left over goes to your estate. Different providers set different age limits but you must be at least 55 or 60 with most schemes to be eligible for a lifetime mortgage. In addition, the value of your home, less any debts secured against it must be in the region of £50,000 and upwards. If you have an existing mortgage you will usually be required to pay this off with the loan. The amounts that you can borrow will vary with your age. The maximum for a roll up loan is usually about half the value.

Reversion schemes

With a reversion scheme you sell part, or all, of your home, but retain the right to live there either rent free or for a token rent. When the home is eventually sold, the reversionary company takes a percentage of the sale proceeds, or the whole amount if you sold 100 per cent of your home. This means that the reversion company, as opposed to the estate gets the benefit of any increase in value of your home. A reversion scheme can be taken out singly or jointly, in which case it continues until the second death.

As with lifetime mortgages, reversion schemes can pay you a single lump sum or a series of smaller lump sums. Alternatively, they may be combined with an annuity or other investment to provide you with a regular income. Investment income is usually

92

taxable but lump sums from the sale of your home are not. The money that you get when you take out the loan will be smaller than the value of the part of your home that you sell. This difference represents the return to the reversionary company. A key factor that the reversionary company uses in deciding what it will offer is how long it expects to have to wait before it gets its money back. To qualify for a reversionary scheme you will usually be between 65-70. Your home must be in reasonable condition and worth a minimum amount, typically £75,000.

Alternatives to equity release

One of the most common reasons for considering equity release is to raise extra income for day-to-day living. If this is your main motive, you might want to consider ensuring that the other avenues for raising income have been explored. For example:

- Are you claiming all the state benefits due to you, such as Pension Credit, Council Tax Benefit and Attendance Allowance
- Have you taken steps to trace any lost pensions that you might be claiming?
- Are you exploiting the potential of your home, for example taking in a lodger?
- Are you making sure that you are not overspending?
- Are you paying too much tax?

You cannot normally use equity release to raise a lump sum of below £10,000. If such a sum is needed you might want to consider taking out an interest only mortgage. Unlike a lifetime mortgage you pay interest each month so the amount borrowed does not grow. The main thing with equity release schemes is that you should get good advice, usually independent advice so that you are totally aware of what it is that you are signing up for.

Selling your home

As we all know, the housing market has undergone changes and the value of property, mainly in the South East has increased out of all proportion. However, the wisdom of using your home, or factoring in your home, as a source of income when retirement age is reached, is questionable.

Property prices are just one of the problems if your intention is to sell up to release capital for your retirement. The other main one is that if you are aiming to downsize to a smaller home then the price of this property may not necessarily be that much cheaper than the family home that you are selling. This does depend of course on the nature, size and value of that property. In addition, there are also the other problems associated with relocating, such as getting used to a new area, neighbours and so on.

You should bear in mind as well that there are significant costs associated with selling, moving and buying. This will eat into any equity that you release from your property and should be taken into account. The good news is that stamp duty payable has decreased for most people. Instead of the 'slab' system, i.e. a one off payment you now pay tax on the amount between property bands. Currently, there is no stamp duty payable on purchases under £500,000. This is due to change on the 1st of July 2021 with the amount reduced to £250,000 and then to £125,000 on October the 1st as it was a temporary measure to stimulate the housing market during the pandemic. Many people say that it has done more harm than good.

Chapter 10

Age Related Extras

Free bus travel in England for older and disabled people

Eligible older and disabled people are entitled to free off-peak travel on local buses anywhere in England. Off peak is between 9.30am to 11pm Monday to Friday and all day weekends and public holidays.

The England bus pass only covers travel in England. It doesn't give you free bus travel in Wales, Scotland or Northern Ireland.

Free bus travel in Wales, Scotland and Northern Ireland

There are similar schemes in each of the above countries and you need to apply to your respective local authorities.

Who is eligible for an older person's bus pass?

If you live in England, you will be entitled to a bus pass when you reach 'eligible age'. If you were born after 5th April 1950, the age you become eligible is tied to the changes in state pension age for women. This affects both men and women.

Women born after 5th April 1950

If you are a woman born after 5th April 1950, you will become eligible for an older persons bus pass when you reach pensionable age.

Men born after 5th April 1950

If you are a man born after 5th April 1950, you will come eligible when you reach the pensionable age of a woman born on the same day.

If you were born before 6th April 1950

You are eligible for an older person's bus pass from your 60th birthday if you were born before 6th April 1950.

Disabled persons bus pass

You are eligible for a disabled person's bus pass if you live in England and are 'eligible disabled'. This means you:

- are blind or partially sighted
- are profoundly or severely deaf
- are without speech
- have a disability, or have suffered an injury, which has a substantial and long term effect on your ability to walk
- don't have arms or have long-term loss of the use of both arms
- have a learning disability

You are also eligible disabled if your application for a driving licence would be refused under section 92 of the Road Traffic Act 1988 (physical fitness). However, you won't be eligible if you were refused because of persistent misuse of drugs or alcohol.

How to get your bus pass

In the first instance you should contact your local council (whether you live in England, Scotland, Ireland or Wales, who will tell you who issues passes in your area.

Bus passes in London-the Freedom Pass

If you are eligible disabled or of eligible age and you live in Greater London, you can apply for a Freedom Pass. This gives you free travel on the entire Transport for London network. On most services, you can use the pass at any time. You can also use your Freedom Pass England-wide, but only during off-peak times outside of London. If you wish to use your bus pass on coaches then you should ask the coach company about terms and conditions. For more about bus passes for elderly and disabled go to www.gov.uk/apply-for-elderly-person-bus-pass

Passport

If you were born on or before 2nd September 1929, you no longer have to pay for your passport. You can ask for a refund if you are eligible and have applied for a replacement passport since 19th May 2004.

Health

NHS Prescriptions. Once you reach age 60 you qualify for free NHS prescriptions (Currently £9.35 in 2021/22). If you are eligible you simply sign the declaration on the back of the prescription. Scotland and Northern Ireland have phased out charges for prescriptions. Prescriptions are already free for all in Wales.

NHS sight tests. From age 60 you also qualify for free NHS sight tests but you still have to pay for the glasses and lenses, unless your income is low. You can get free sight tests from age 40 if you are considered at risk of developing glaucoma because a close family member has this condition (or any age if you already have sight problems).

Help with bills

Winter fuel payments. This scheme is in force all over the UK and provides a cash sum to every household with one or more people over 60 in the 'qualifying week' which is the week beginning the third Monday in September. You can use the cash in any way you like. However, it is designed specifically to help you cope with Winter fuel bills. The standard payment is normally between £100-£300 depending on your situation. If you want more details concerning this payment you should go to www.directgov.co.uk.

Free or discounted Television licence.

You can get either:

- a free TV licence if you're 75 or over and you get Pension Credit
- a discount if you're blind or in residential care

If you're 75 or over

You can get a free TV licence if you're 75 or older and you either:

- get Pension Credit
- live with your partner who gets Pension Credit

The licence covers everyone living at your address.

You can apply when you're 74 if you already get Pension Credit. You'll still need to pay for your licence until the end of the month before your 75th birthday. After that you'll be covered by your free licence.

How to apply

You can apply for a free licence online.

You can also apply by phone.

TV Licensing

Telephone: 0300 790 6071

Minicom: 0300 709 6050

If you're in residential care

You can get a special licence for £7.50 if you live in an eligible residential care home. You must be either:

- retired and over 60
- disabled

Your housing manager can apply for you.

If you're registered blind

You can get a 50% discount if you're registered blind or live with someone who is. The licence must be in the blind person's name - if it's not, you can make a new application to transfer it into their name. You'll need to provide your existing TV licence number when you apply.

Your home

You can get help with heating and fuel efficiency if you are aged 60 or over. You should go to: www.gov.uk/browse/benefits/heating.

Repairs and Improvements

One of the most important elements of your home is that of its condition. When you retire or are close to retiring, this presents the ideal opportunity to assess the overall condition of your home and to draw up a condition survey (or have one drawn up) so that you can plan expenditure. It is wise to commence the work as soon as possible after retirement, or before if possible, so that you can still carry out works yourself, without resorting to using building firms. This will save money and mean that you have more control. This chapter also points the way to the various agencies that exist who will give you advice on repairs and maintenance and also funding.

Deciding what needs to be carried out

There are specialist advice agencies, called Home Improvement Agencies (sometimes called Care and Repair or Staying Put) that will give specialist advice to older and vulnerable householders and also to people living in private rented accommodation. They are small scale, no-for-profit organisations, usually managed locally by housing associations, councils or charities. They will usually offer practical help with tasks such as arranging a condition survey, getting estimates from builders (trusted builders) applying for grants or loans and also keeping an eye on the progress of work. They may charge a fee towards their assistance, which is usually included in the grant or loans that you may be in receipt of.

To find out whether there is a home improvement agency in your area, you should contact your local Age UK or the local council housing department or Foundations (the National Co-ordinating Body for Home Improvement Agencies). Address at the rear of the book.

If there is no Home Improvement Agency in your area you might want to engage a surveyor to carry one out for you. As these are costly, or can be, you should always ask what the cost will be first. The Chartered Surveyor Voluntary Service exists to help people who would other wise be able to get professional advice. You need to be referred to them by a Citizens Advice Bureau first.

Finding a Builder

If there is no Home Improvement Agency in your area, you should take care, great care, when trying to find a good reliable builder. We have all heard stories of rogue builders who carry out shoddy work and charge over the odds. If you intend to employ a builder, particularly for a larger job, then you should always employ a builder backed by a proper guarantee scheme. The Federation of Master Builders (FMB) offers a MasterBond Warranty: its members must meet certain criteria and adhere to the FMB's Code of Practice. The ten-year insurance backed warranty will add 1.5% to the total cost of a job but is money well spent.

Information on this scheme can be obtained from the FMB website at www.fmb.org.uk. To ensure that you get a good job done, the FMB recommends that you:

- Always ask for references and names of previous clients
- Get estimates from two or three builders
- Ask for the work to be covered by an insurance backed warranty
- Get a written specification and quotation
- Use a contract (the FMB has a plain English contract for small works)
- Agree any staged and final payments before a job
- Avoid dealing in cash

The FMB has played a leading role in the development of the government backed TrustMark scheme, which is a consumer protection initiative for the home repair and improvement sector.

A wide range of traders, including plumbers and electricians, are being licensed to become TrustMark registered firms. For more information contact TrustMark. Address at the rear of this book.

Financial help with repairs and improvements

Sometimes, individuals find themselves in a position where they cannot afford repairs to their homes. There are, however, various forms of assistance at hand. Local authorities have general powers to provide help with repairs and also adaptations to housing. The assistance isn't always cash based, it can also be provided in the form of labour material or advice. The cash element will usually be either grants or loans. Local authorities will have published policies explaining the various forms of assistance. These can vary from time to time, as many of them are dependant on national legislation and government funding. Below are a few of the types of grants available.

Disabled facilities grant

These grants provide facilities and adaptations to help a disabled person to live as independently and in as much comfort as possible. They are means tested (i.e.) dependant on income, with the exception of grants for disabled children. For more information you should go to www.gov.uk/disabled-facilities-grants

If you receive Pension credit, Income Support or Income based jobseekers allowance, you may be able to get a Community Care Grant or Budgeting Loan from the Social fund to help you with the cost of minor repairs. Social services departments provide funding for some minor adaptation works. They may also be able to help with some types of work not covered by the disabled facilities grant.

If you want to raise capital from your home to pay for works, the Home Improvement Trust may be able to help. It is a not-for-profit company that has links with a number of commercial lenders who provide older people with low cost loans raised against the value of their home. You can contact Home Improvement Trust direct at the address at the rear of the book.

The Care and Repair England publication also provides useful information about organising and financing building works. You can get a copy by phoning 0115 950 6500 or by downloading it from the website www.careandrepair-england.org.uk.

Adapting your home

You may need to make certain adaptations to your home if you or a member of your family needs them, such as mobility aids, to make it easier to navigate the house. There are other areas that can be helpful, such as the positioning of the furniture. Occupational Therapists can give detailed advice. They can assess a persons mobility and their ability to move around and can provide appropriate advice. You should contact your local social services department and ask for an assessment of needs. You don't have to have a letter from the doctor but this can speed things up. Social services should provide some equipment free if you or a relative is assessed as needing them. All minor adaptations costing less than £1000 must be provided free of charge.

For full information about special equipment and furniture, contact the Disabled Living Foundation at the address at the rear of the book.

Ch. 11

Care Options For the Future

As is well documented over a third of people over 65-74 and over a half over the age of 75 have a long-standing health condition that affects their lives in some way. The ability to carry on living in ones own home really depends a lot on the availability of appropriate care. Quite often this is not readily available, and comes at a cost. Those who are fortunate enough can be cared for by their family.

In 1993, the government introduced policies designed to help more people live independently in their own homes through the expansion of formal support services. This has had the effect of reducing the number of people who need care home support.

However, we are living in an age of an increasing elderly population and there is increase pressure on finances and the ability of government to pay. Whether you are thinking of support in the future for an aging relative or indeed for yourself, there are several main factors that you need to consider and decisions to be made:

- Exactly what form of care might be needed in the future, whether a retirement home or higher level sheltered housing
- Where will the money come from to pay for the care?

For more information about care homes and costs and fees in Scotland go to:

ttps://www.caresourcer.com/caresupport/financing-care/care-home-fees...
For Northern Ireland go to:
https://www.nidirect.gov.uk/paying-your-residential-care-or...
We need now to examine the various options available.

Care in the home

Most people would rather stay in their own home and receive the appropriate level of support for their needs. Regardless of your own personal financial situation you have the right to approach social services in your local authority area for a needs assessment. Then a manager from the department will visit you in your home (or relative as case may be) and put together a care plan for you.

The whole approach to care in the home and care in residential homes has been redefined by the Care Act 2014, a summary of which is below.

The Care Act 2014

The Care Act 2014 came into force on 1st April 2015 along with a range of new supporting regulations and a single set of statutory guidance, which, taken together, describe how the Act should be applied in practice. The aim of the change was to simplify and modernise the system, which had become very complex and also to create a new approach to charging. The Care Act 2014l actually came into force in two stages, in April 2015 and April 2016. Some of the key changes introduced in 2015 were:

- The promotion of individual well-being as an overarching principle within all the activities of a local authority including: assessment, eligibility, prevention, means testing and care and support planning.

- New national eligibility criterion for both the adult requesting services and their carer(s) leading to rights to services and based around the well-being principle. The previous four local eligibility levels have now become one, set at approximately the previous 'substantial' level. Carers now have an absolute right to have their assessed, eligible, support needs met for the first time; they have a slightly different eligibility criterion to the service user, but are subject to the same means test rules.

- A person-centred, outcomes-focussed, approach to assessing and meeting needs. Local authorities must consider how to meet each person's specific needs rather than simply considering what existing service they will fit into. They must also consider what someone wants/needs to achieve or do and the effect on them of any difficulties they are having.

- The whole system is now administered via personal budgets and based on the principles of the personalisation policy that has been developed over the past few years.

- A 'right to request' service provision for a fee where someone with eligible needs is found to be a self-funder (must pay the whole cost of a service) in the means test. This right does not exist for care home provision.

- New local authority 'market shaping' duties to ensure adequate, diverse, good quality, local service provision.

- The duty to prevent, reduce and delay the need for services and also related duties to integrate care with the NHS where this benefits a service user.

- A lifetime care cost cap (£72,000 in 2021) above which the State will meet the cost of paying a person's eligible social care needs. The national cap will be reviewed every five years. (keep an eye on this as there have been attempts to change the goal posts and U turns)
- (Currently, in 2021, the government has considered both Sir Andrew Dilnot's 2001 report, Commission on Funding of Care and Support, and the Health and Social Care Committee's 2020 report Social Care: Funding and Workforce. which looks at all aspects of care costs. The report recommends a reduction of care costs and a lifetime cap of £46,000).
- The introduction of care accounts, which will require a local authority to track a person's personal expenditure towards meeting their eligible social care needs, towards the new care cost cap –based on the amount set out in their personal budget. Each account will be adjusted annually in line with the national rise in average earnings. Some local authorities may start to assess for care accounts ahead of the April 2016 start date to avoid capacity issues.
- Independent personal budgets for those people with assessed, eligible, needs but who have capital in excess of the upper threshold and who are meeting the cost of their care and support themselves. This is a choice that will be available to enable payments to be noted in the person's care account.

There are a wide range of support services that can be provided to help you stay in your own home and also to assist your carer if you have one. Services could include: domiciliary (home) carer and personal assistants; meals delivered at home; day center attendance and respite care; live-in care services; rehabilitation services; sheltered accommodation and supported living; shared lives services; other housing options; community support; counseling; direct payment support organisations; information, brokerage and advice services1.

Other forms of assistance could include the provision of specialist disability equipment, adaptations to your home, community alarms and other types of assistive technology.

For more detailed and specific information about the changes and new criteria introduced in the Care Act you should go to www.ageuk.org.uk they have ready prepared fact sheets which will help you to see what you are entitled to.

There are certain fundamental rules that local authorities must abide by. Charges should not reduce the income that a person has left below a set level. If a person is 60 or over, this is the Pension Credit Guarantee credit level plus a buffer which is dependant where you live in the UK, for example 25% in England and 35% in Wales. The assessment should be based only on your income and generally not that of your partner or anyone else. If you feel that you are paying too much for your care services then you have the right to ask the local authority to review your financial assessment.

How the care is paid for
Either the local authority will pay you direct in cash for your services or, if you so desire, you can ask the local authority to arrange and pay for the care. The Government has also introduced a scheme called Individual Budgets, arising out of the Care Act 2014, which are similar to Direct Payment, so you receive a cash sum, but it covers a wide range of services so it includes, for example, help towards a warden in sheltered

housing. The aim of cash payments is to put the individual in more control of the services that they buy. Obviously, this may not be suited to everyone and some people will be more reliant on the local authority to provide and pay for services.

Other benefits available

There are other benefits available such as personal independence payment (replacing Disability Living allowance for those up to age 64) or if you are over 65 Attendance Allowance. These benefits are tax-free and are not means tested. If you are a carer, you will also have the right to a free needs assessment to pay for extra levels of need.

The care plan devised by the local authority might for example recommend that someone be paid for sitting with a relative whilst you have a few hours off, or respite care (where the disabled person moves temporarily into a care home). You will be expected to pay for these services unless your income and savings are low .

Retirement housing

Retirement housing is known by a number of different names that usually reflects the level of care needed, for example sheltered housing, warden assisted housing or warden controlled housing. This is designed for people over 60 (sometimes can be 55). Usually, it is a scheme that comprises a number of flats and maybe a few bungalows with communal areas for residents, such as lounge and gardens and in some cases a kitchen for the provision of communal meals. There is also usually a laundry area and an emergency call system plus a warden if included in the overall scheme cost.

Some schemes are private, people buy a lease, known as leasehold schemes for the elderly. Sheltered housing to rent is normally provided by local authorities and, more usually now, housing associations. To qualify for these schemes you have to prove that you are in need and cannot afford to buy. You may qualify for Housing Benefit.

The main cost associated with retirement housing, whether rented or owned, is the service charge. As an ex-care home manager myself, I have long experience of the difficulties that surround service charges.

The service charge covers the cost of wardens, communal areas, emergency call system and gardening. Many other areas are included. If you are on a low income then you might be eligible for housing benefit for some of the services.

Ordinary sheltered housing does not include care services, this has to be arranged with your local authority. However, as discussed, sheltered housing can be more intensive and the levels of charges will reflect this. For example do you, or a relative envisage needing intensive care of a kind provided by category one sheltered housing or will you need a lesser degree of care?

Moving to a care home

If you move to a care home to receive personal care you may have to pay some or all of the fees yourself, depending on your income. If your main aim is health care, the NHS should pay. This is called NHS continuing care. In some circumstances, you may receive care at home either to avoid admission to hospital or to enable you to leave hospital early. In this case, you are entitled to free care-called intermediate care-which may include a mix of health and social care. The social care element should be free for a maximum of six weeks.

If your primary reason for moving to a care home is for help with personal care such as getting up, going to bed, bathing and so on, in general you are expected to pay for the fees yourself unless your income and savings are low. In that case, the local authority will carry out a financial assessment to determine whether you should pay anything at all. This assessment is in line with the capital limits which can be obtained from your local authority.

Even if your main need is personal care, you may require some nursing care as well and this is provided free, up to set limits depending where you live in the UK and, in England, on the extent of the nursing care that you need.

The Government pays these sums direct to your care provider. If you are paying for your care home fees yourself, you are likely to qualify for Attendance Allowance. If the NHS or local authority is paying for some or all of the fees, you will not be able to get Attendance Allowance as well.

As described above, the Care Act 2014 has affected the way in which home care and care home funding is allocated and you should contact Age UK to find out more.

Assessing your finances

Whether or not you can get state funding depends in part on how much capital you have (means testing). Capital includes savings and investments but can also include your house, However, if your partner (married or not), an elderly or disabled relative or a child under 16 still lives there, the value of your home is disregarded. The local authority also has the discretion to ignore your home, if, for example, you carer will carry on living there.

How will my capital be treated in the means test?

You capital is the phrase used to describe the total amount of your savings, any property you own and any shares you might have. It does not include your pension and benefits you might be getting. There are also some national differences. In Wales for example, there's a cap on the maximum you'll have to pay. While in Scotland, care services are free up to a specified limit.

For the UK the below are the capital limits:

Region	Upper savings threshold for any local authority funding in 2020-21	Lower savings threshold for maximum local authority funding in 2020-21
England	£23,250	£14,250
Wales	£24,000 (care at home) or £50,000 (care in a care home)	£24,000 (care at home) or £50,000 (care in a care home)
Scotland	£28,500	£18,000
Northern Ireland	£23,250	£14,250

**

If you are a couple, the local authority is not allowed to base the financial assessment on your joint resources. It must consider only the capital and income that belongs to you. If you are holding assets on behalf of someone else you must prove that they are not your assets or the local authority will treat them as your assets. You can be treated as still owning capital if you are deemed to have deliberately deprived yourself of it. This could be the case if you have given away assets to other family members in advance of applying for a care assessment. Spouses and civil partners are in law liable to support each other and can be asked to contribute towards fees, but the local authority should not do this if it would cause financial hardship. The local authority cannot ask an unmarried partner or other family member to contribute.

How much will I have to pay?

After the means test the local authority should give you a written record of their decision of what you will have to pay and what they will pay, and how they calculated it. You should not be left with less than £29.30 (2021/2022) a week after any contribution to your fees. This is known as your Personal Expenses Allowance.

What if I run out of money?

If you are paying fees yourself (called self-funding) and your capital goes down to less than £23,250, the local authority may assist with funding. You should request an assessment a few months before that happens. They should arrange one as soon as possible so you don't have to use up your capital below that amount.

Planning ahead for care

If you think that you will need care for a long time, taking out a long-term care product could work out cheaper than the fees. Planning ahead is very difficult and there is no real way to know what your needs will be. There are a few providers of long-term care products and these tend to be expensive. One obvious route is to take out some form of insurance. In the UK, there is just one provider of long-term care insurance. It targets healthy individuals aged 50-70 years. With high premiums (for example around £100 per month for a policy that would pay out a flat rate of £1000 a month it is easy to see why the take up of this insurance is limited.

A handful of providers offer what is known as impaired life annuities that you buy at the point when you need care. You pay a lump sum and in return get an income that pays all or a substantial part of your care costs. The income is tax-free provided that it is paid direct to the provider. The amount that you pay for the annuity will depend on the monthly payments that you need and also the annuity providers assessment of how long that it will have to pay out.

****

Ch. 12

Income Tax and Retirement

Income Tax

Regardless of whether we are employed, retired or self-employed, we all have to accept the fact that HMRC are going to take a percentage of our income in the form of income tax and there is nothing we can do to avoid it.

The retired, employed and self-employed are treated in slightly different ways and therefore we shall look at each individually, once we have assessed the structure of income tax. You should check your current tax allowances with HM Revenue and Customs as they are subject to annual change. For more information about tax and state and other pensions see chapter 9 onwards

Personal allowance

Most people are allowed to receive a certain amount of income before tax is payable. This is known as the basic personal allowance. In 2021/2022 allowances are:

Band	Taxable income	Tax rate
Personal Allowance	Up to £12,570	0%
Basic rate	£12,571 to £50,270	20%
Higher rate	£50,271 to £150,000	40%
Additional rate	over £150,000	45%

You don't get a Personal Allowance on taxable income over £125,140.

Income above £100,000

If your income is above £100,000, basic personal allowance is further reduced by £1 for each £2 earned over the £100,000 limit, irrespective of age.

Blind person's allowance

You may also be entitled to an additional allowance if you or your spouse or registered civil partner are blind or have severely impaired sight. This is another full relief allowance as it is treated in the same way as the personal allowance, so increases the amount of income you can receive before you start to pay tax. In 2021-22 this allowance is £2,520.

In England and Wales

If you live in England or Wales, you will need to be certified as blind and appear on a local authority register of blind people to claim this allowance.

In Scotland and Northern Ireland

If you have not been certified as blind and live in Scotland or Northern Ireland you will qualify for the allowance if your eyesight is so bad that you are unable to perform any work where your eyesight is essential.

Unused balance

If your income is not enough to make use of the allowance, any unused balance can be transferred to your spouse or registered civil partner. Married couples get certain tax breaks.

Married couple's allowance

You only qualify for this allowance if you or your husband, wife or registered civil partner were born before 6 April 1935. Unlike the personal allowance, the married couple's allowance is not an amount you can earn before you start paying tax. Instead, it's a restricted relief allowance, which means the tax you pay is reduced by deducting 10% of the allowance from your final tax bill.

Marriage transferable tax allowance

Additionally, from April 2021, married couples born after 1935 will be able to transfer up to £1,260 of unused personal allowance (Marriage transferable tax allowance).

Claiming maintenance relief

You can claim this relief for certain maintenance payments you make if you or your ex-spouse or registered civil partner were born before 6 April 1935 and you pay the maintenance under a legally binding agreement. It works in a similar way to the married couple's allowance. Your tax bill will be reduced by 10% of the maintenance relief allowance or the amount you pay in maintenance, if that amount is lower.

The Employed

If you are employed your tax affairs are conducted on the fiscal year or financial year which is 6th April to 5th April the following year. You are taxed on what is known as Schedule E (Pay As You Earn) which means that both tax and national insurance will be deducted by your employer before you receive your salary. You therefore receive your salary net of tax. This is without doubt the simplest way to conduct your tax affairs as there is very little further communication you need to have, if any, with your tax office.

At the end of the financial year you will receive a P60 which is a statement of your full year's earnings and it will contain details of how much tax and national insurance you have paid as well as pension contributions if you are in an occupational pension scheme.

You should always keep your P60 in a safe place as it often requested by banks and building societies for mortgage or loan purposes.

If you work for a large employer you may receive fringe benefits such as a company car, mortgage subsidy, or private medical insurance. These are very worthwhile benefits but you must remember they are also taxable benefits which will mean that your personal allowance will reduce to account for the real value of these benefits. If you have such benefits but notice your tax code hasn't changed then it is your responsibility to inform your tax office, as failure to do so may mean that in future years they could claim payment for undisclosed benefits.

Not all benefits are taxable, however, and the most attractive one is obviously a company pension scheme. In recent years a great deal of companies have moved towards Performance Related Pay. When you leave employment you will be provided with a P45 which is similar to a P60 but is for the benefit of your new employer to use in order to calculate your earnings to date and therefore make the necessary stoppages in your salary. It is always worthwhile taking a copy of your P45 for your own reference.

The self-employed

If you are self employed your own tax year can be any period of 12 months you want. In the eyes of the Inland Revenue you will be taxed on what is known as Schedule D and pay Class 2 National Insurance contributions. Being self employed means that the money you receive for the services you provide will be gross and therefore no tax will have been deducted.

It is advisable that you keep an accurate record of all the money you receive and receipts for any money you spend in connection with your business activities. At the beginning of April you would normally receive a tax return form which explores all the potential sources of income you may have. This must be duly signed and returned within a month.

A large percentage of the self employed use the services of an accountant, as they best know the ways in which your tax liability can be reduced and their services certainly make it easier if you are self-employed and are hoping to take out a mortgage.

HM Revenue and Customs will negotiate with you or your accountant once they have details of your year's earnings and business expenses. Once the expenses have been taken from the gross figure this will leave your net income and therefore the amount upon which you will be expected to pay tax.

Your tax liability is normally paid in 2 instalments, the first on 1st January and the second on the 1st July. The Inland Revenue, however, do not wait for your accounts to be completed and in most cases you will be expected to make instalments based on assessments of your expected income and once your accounts are finalised you will then be informed of any over or under payment.

Tax and pensions

You pay tax if your total annual income adds up to more than your Personal Allowance. Your total income could include:

- the State Pension you get (either the basic State Pension or the new State Pension)
- Additional State Pension
- a private pension (workplace or personal) - you can take some of this tax-free
- earnings from employment or self-employment
- any taxable benefits you get
- any other income, such as money from investments, property or savings

You may have to pay Income Tax at a higher rate if you take a large amount from a private pension. You may also owe extra tax at the end of the tax year.

Lifetime allowance

You usually pay a tax charge if the total value of your private pensions is more than £1,073,100 (Lifetime allowance). Your pension provider will take off the charge before you get your payment.

Tax if someone inherits your pension

Other rules apply if someone inherits your State pension or your private pension. You won't usually pay any tax if your total annual income adds up to less than your Personal Allowance.

Lump sums from your pension

You can usually take up to 25% of the amount built up in any pension as a tax-free lump sum. The tax-free lump sum doesn't affect your Personal Allowance. Tax is taken off the remaining amount before you get it.

Example:

Your whole pension is worth £60,000. You take £15,000 tax-free. Your pension provider takes tax off the remaining £45,000. When you can take your pension depends on your pension's rules. It's usually 55 at the earliest. You might have to pay Income Tax at a higher rate if you take a large amount from your pension. You could also owe extra tax at the end of the tax year.

How you can take your pension

A pension worth up to £10,000

You can usually take any pension worth up to £10,000 in one go. This is called a 'small pot' lump sum. If you take this option, 25% is tax-free.

You can usually get:

- up to 3 small pot lump sums from different personal pensions
- unlimited small pot lump sums from different workplace pensions

A pension worth up to £30,000 that includes a defined benefit pension

If you have £30,000 or less in all of your private pensions, you can usually take everything you have in your defined benefit pension as a 'trivial commutation' lump sum. If you take this option, 25% is tax-free. If this lump sum is paid from more than one pension, you must:

- have your savings in each scheme valued by the provider on the same day, no more than 3 months before you get the first payment
- get all payments within 12 months of the first payment

If you take payments from a pension before taking the rest as a lump sum, you pay tax on the whole lump sum.

Cash from a defined contribution pension

Check with your provider about how you can take money from a defined contribution pension. You can take:

- all the money built up in your pension as cash - up to 25% is tax-free
- smaller cash sums from your pension - up to 25% of each sum is tax-free

You may have to pay a tax charge on money you put into your pension after you withdraw cash.

If your life expectancy is less than a year

You may be able to take all the money in your pension as a tax-free lump sum, if all of the following apply:

- you're expected to live less than a year because of serious illness
- you're under 75
- you don't have more than the lifetime allowance of £1 million in pension savings

If you're over 75 you'll pay Income Tax on the lump sum. Check with your pension provider. Some pension funds will keep at least 50% of your pension for your spouse or civil partner.

Capital Gains Tax

If you have successfully bought and sold investments, antiques and property etc., you may find that you would be liable for capital gains tax. Everyone is allowed to make a profit on opportunities that they fund with their own capital. There is, however, a limit, which you should check with HMRC, and any profit/gain that exceeds that figure would be liable for capital gains tax at the individual's marginal rate.

Tax on dividends

You may get a dividend payment if you own shares in a company. In April 2021/22, the first £2,000 is tax free.

Above this allowance the tax you pay depends on which Income Tax band you're in. Add your income from dividends to your other taxable income when working this out. You may pay tax at more than one rate.

Tax band	Tax rate on dividends over £2,000
Basic rate	7.5%
Higher rate	32.5%
Additional rate	38.1%

Inheritance Tax

The subject of death is one which is rarely discussed openly and inheritance tax is thought to be an issue that is largely limited to the wealthy. This however, is a misconception, as inheritance tax will affect more people now than ever before. In order to establish whether you are going to have an inheritance tax bill, you must assess the total value of the estate left by the deceased. This would include all assets and any gifts made within the preceding seven years. If the total figure exceeds £325.000 (2021-22) there will be a liability on the surplus of 40%. If the estate totals less than £325,000 there will be no liability. You should check these limits with HMRC as they are subject to change. It now becomes clear that if you have been able to build a reasonable amount of savings, paid off your mortgage and may have received a pension lump sum and an inheritance yourself, you could be bordering on the £325,000 limit and your estate would be liable for inheritance tax. You should not restrict your own lifestyle in order to reduce your beneficiaries' tax bill but if you can afford it there are various options and exemptions that could substantially reduce the future liability.

Exemptions

1. There is no inheritance tax between husband and wife.

2. To a U.K charity.

3. Gifts that total £3,000 a year.

4. £250 gifts made to anyone and however many people you like. This cannot be given to the same people as the £3,000.

5. Wedding presents, £5,000 from a parent, £2,500 from a grandparent, £1,000 from friend or family.

6. Part of a divorce settlement.

7. To support female parent-in-law if she is divorced, widowed or separated.

8. Selected agricultural land or business assets and unquoted shares.

Gifts made seven years before death

Any gifts that the deceased made in the last 7 years of his or her life will be liable to inheritance tax on a sliding scale and the value of the gift will also form part of the estate. In order to reduce the liability you could write any life insurance policies you have under trust and should you die, the benefits of your policies would not form part of your estate, but be payable to your spouse or children, therefore avoiding possible inheritance tax. For more detailed advice on taxation you should go to the HMRC website at www.hmrc.gov.uk

****

Ch. 13

Writing an Effective Will

It is often said that the toughest job in sales is to get people to buy fire extinguishers: no one wants to think that they and their family could be caught in a fire which could kill or injure. The same thinking seems to apply to making a will: most people in Britain have not made a will- something which their families could well come to regret.

There are two sorts of people for whom making a will is not just a good idea, but essential: Anyone who is reasonably well off or whose affairs are at all complicated, and anyone who is in a partnership. Unmarried partners (or outside a civil arrangement) cannot inherit from each other unless there is a will: your partner could end up with nothing when you die, unless they can show that they were financially dependent.

There is no such thing in England as a 'common-law marriage.'

The State moves in

- When anyone dies without making a will, the law, i.e. the state, takes over. In the extreme case, where you die single and have no other surviving relatives, all your estate could end up with the Crown. And the law is not at all generous to your spouse: if you have no children If there are no surviving children, grandchildren or great-grandchildren, the partner will inherit:

- all the personal property and belongings of the person who has died and
- the whole of the estate with interest from the date of death.

If there are children, the widow/widower will get £270,000, plus personal assets and income from 50% of the rest; the children will get 50% when they reach age 18 and the other 50% when the surviving parents dies. If you aim to save inheritance tax, you need to make a will. For 2021-22 the 'nil rate band' is fixed at £325,000 which means that no tax is due below that level, and anything more is taxed at 40%.

How to make a will

So how do you make a will? You can draw up your own using a will-making kit which you can buy from a big stationer or download from the net. That represents the most cost-effective choice and it could work if your affairs are reasonably straightforward. But if you think that your will could be disputed, i.e. subject to legal challenge, then you need to go to a solicitor.

That will be a few hundred pounds well spent and you may qualify for legal aid on financial grounds or because of age: you could ask Citizens Advice. You will probably know a solicitor or have employed one in a recent property deal. You will talk to friends or you can contact the Law Society for a list of solicitors near where you live.

Put yourself on paper

Before you go to your solicitor, there are two important things you need to do. Firstly, you need to put yourself on paper - everything you own that is of significant size, including cars, jewelry, property, home contents, bank accounts, shares and life insurance. At the same time, you put down all that you owe, such as mortgage, overdraft and credit card debts. You need to give precise details of the beneficiaries and be very specific about what you are leaving them.

The second thing you need to do is choose an executor, one or two people whose job is to ensure that your wishes are carried out. Your first thought may be someone younger than you (you will need their agreement to act) but there is no guarantee that they will outlive you. If no executor has been designated, the state will appoint a solicitor for you - for a fee. If you go to a solicitor, think about a formula, e.g. a partner appointed by whoever is senior partner of the firm at the time. The executors will need to know where your will is kept, with your solicitor or in your bank.

Time to revisit?

You have made your will, but you should resolve to look at it again, say every five years: people change, as do assets and liabilities. It is a good basic rule to revisit your will when a new child arrives or when you move house. Outside events can change a will: if you were single when you drew up your will, it may become invalid if you get married. But divorce or separation do not make a will invalid, so you might want to make changes. If you just want to make minor alterations, you can add supplementary changes known

128

as codicils. These are added separately and all alterations have to be properly witnessed. If the alterations are significant, you will need to make a new will which will revoke any other wills you have made.

The case for making a will is essentially simple: as Benjamin Franklin said, death and taxes are certain, and making a will means that your family will not have to spend time and energy sorting out a complicated financial and legal set-up. But when you look beyond middle age you have to assess probabilities - you may be out of the country when your signature is needed, you may get ill or you may be injured. We are now talking power of attorney.

Power of attorney

You probably gave your solicitor a power of attorney when you sold your flat; you may have given a power of attorney to your partner when you had to go on an overseas business trip but wanted to buy some shares in the UK. A power of attorney simply gives a person the power to act for somebody else in their financial affairs or in health and personal welfare. (Rules in Scotland are different). The power of attorney you gave your solicitor was probably an ordinary power of attorney, created for a set period of time and for a specific piece of business. That all seems very practical, you may think, but why should you give anyone a power of attorney? The short answer is that if you are away or fall ill, you will need someone to look after your affairs - and that requires a power of attorney. (If this happens and you had not given a power of attorney, your friends and relatives would have to go to court, which would take time and cost money)

Ending the power

When you have given a power of attorney, there are two ways in which it can be ended. You can end it yourself by using a deed of revocation or it will end automatically if you, the donor, lose 'mental capacity.' This is where problems can arise. Suppose you gave your partner an ordinary power of attorney to handle your bank account while you go on your overseas business trip; you are mugged while on your trip and lie unconscious in hospital. Your power of attorney is ended because you are mentally out of action; for the same reason you cannot give a new power of attorney. Your partner cannot legally access your bank account or have any involvement in your affairs: catch 22? The answer to this puzzle was to create an Enduring Power of Attorney. Under an EPA when you were mugged on your overseas trip, your partner and/or solicitor would register with the court and they could then act on your behalf. New EPAs cannot be created since October 2007.

New lasting powers

EPA's have been replaced by Lasting Powers of Attorney which have separate sections for personal welfare and for property and affairs. Each of these has to be registered separately and the LP A can only be used - similar to an EPA - once it has been registered with the Office of the Public Guardian. If you want to change your mind, you can cancel all the different Powers of Attorney, so long as you are still mentally capable. This may all sound elaborate but it represents the only answer to the situation where you cannot manage your affairs because of accident, illness, age or whatever - but someone needs to do so.

The need for a power of attorney is now that much greater because banks and financial institutions are more aware of their legal responsibilities. Formerly, a friendly bank manager might have been prepared to help your partner sort out what needed to be done while you were out of action. Now, your friendly bank manager is more likely to stick to the legal rules, if only to protect himself and his employer.

You as attorney

One of your colleagues may ask you to be his attorney; if you agree, make sure that a firm of solicitors are also involved. You will have some costs - such as when you register the power of attorney - and there are strict rules, for keeping money and property separate and for keeping accounts of any dealings for the person who gave you the power. When you register, you are obliged to tell your colleague's relatives who are free to object. This is not a job for a layman acting all by himself

****

PART 3
FINANCE AND
INVESTMENTS

Chapter 14

Seeking Financial Advice

When considering retirement finances, it is essential to have a general understanding about the current investment landscape, which includes personal savings and also longer term investments such as the stock market. One thing is certain, it is essential to ensure that your money is safe and increases in value.

It may be that you will seek financial advice and below we start with the role of financial advisors, as this is an area where you can easily go wrong.

Financial Advice and Financial Advisors

There are many ways to purchase financial products nowadays, either through the Internet or by telephone. However, when considering more complex financial issues, it is evident that professional advice is needed. There are numerous advantages to using financial advisors, one of the main ones being that you will have extra protection if things go wrong. The first step towards finding a good advisor is considering which type is likely to provide the service you need. Like solicitors and other professionals, financial advisors do specialise and you would have to find the correct advisor for your needs. It is also very important to discover whether or not the advisor is properly authorised and registered and approved by the correct bodies. Nowadays, advisors and the companies that they work for must be authorised by the financial services watchdog, the Financial Conduct Authority (FCA). The FCA is responsible for the conduct of advisors. To be on the safe side you should always check with the FCA. You can also find out what type of business the advisor is authorised to do. These details are held on the FCA's register. Its public enquiries helpline is on 0800 111 6768.

Stockbrokers

Stockbrokers have become more accessible over the years, particularly recently. Many of the newer telephone based services cater mainly for investors who know which shares they want to buy and sell, and they do not provide advice other than general information bulletins. However, many firms still offer advisory and discretionary management services. For smaller investors, a unit or investment manage trust management may be offered.

To find out which stockbrokers offer these services to private clients, contact the Association of Private Client Investment Managers and Stockbrokers (APCIMS). It has a free directory of member firms, many of which provide a full financial planning service. See appendix for details.

Complaints

If you are unhappy with a financial product or service, you have the means to complain. As with many complaints, you must first give the company the chance to put things right. If this cannot be achieved then there are other routes, such as the Financial Ombudsman Service.

However, before the Ombudsman will take up your complaint you must be able to show that you have followed the company complaint procedure and have still received no satisfactory solution to your problem.

Complaints schemes generally

The Financial Ombudsman Service. This provides a single complaints scheme divided into three specialist divisions for banking and loans, insurance and investments. It covers the following types of companies and organisations:

- Banks
- Building societies
- Financial advisors
- Firms dealing in futures and options/ Friendly Societies
- Fund managers
- Life insurance companies
- Pension providers
- Stockbrokers

The Pensions Advisory Service. PAS provides initial advice and conciliation for complaints about employers pension schemes.

The Pensions Ombudsman. This ombudsman decides on complaints relating to employers pension schemes not resolved by OPAS.

The General Insurance Standards Council. This is a voluntary scheme handling complaints about general insurance brokers such as those selling motor and household cover.

The Property Ombudsman Scheme. This is a voluntary scheme dealing with complaints about estate agents from both buyers and sellers. All estate agents are required to register with some sort of Estate Agents Redress Scheme approved by the Office of Fair Trading..

Protection

If you lose money due to miss selling or misadministration, an ombudsman may be able to ensure that you get financial compensation. However, if fraud is apparent, this may not be possible, or if the company or individual becomes bankrupt.

The Financial Services Compensation Scheme
The maximum amounts of compensation are as follows:

Deposits
£85,000 per person per firm
100% of first £85,000
Investments
£85,000 per person per firm
100% of first £85,000
Home (e.g. Mortgage advisors and arrangements)
£85,,000 per person per firm
100% of first £85,000

Pensions
If the firm failed after 1st April 2019 you will be paid 100% of your claim with no upper limit. If your SIPP provider fails up to 85% of your claim is paid per individual per firm. If you have received bad pension advice you could be eligible to win compensation up to 85% per person per firm.

Insurance business
If you bought your insurance policy from an insurance firm that's failed, and you bought your insurance after 8th October 2020 the kind of insurance you have and when the firm failed will affect how much compensation you could claim.
100% protected:
• Compulsory insurance
• Long-term insurance

- Professional indemnity insurance
- Claims arising from the death or incapacity of the policyholder due to injury, sickness or infirmity
- Building guarantee policies
- 90% protected:
- All other kinds of insurance

There are different rules for insurance purchased before October 2020 and for further advice on all compensation schemes you should go to the Financial Services Compensation Scheme website at fscs.org.uk.

Fraud Compensation Fund run by the Pension Protection Fund
This covers member liabilities of occupational pensions in full.

Offshore compensation
Investors should bear in mind that these schemes do not apply to firms based outside the United Kingdom. Although some offshore investment centres, such as the Isle of Man, may have their own compensation schemes, others do not. When investing outside the UK take great care to gain as much information as possible from the institution concerned.

****

Chapter 15

Insurance-General Advice

Life Insurance

The concept of life insurance is by no means a 20th century development. The earliest forms can be traced back to Greek and Roman times. Clubs would be formed and, for a regular contribution, a lump sum would be paid in the event of death of an individual.

In today's society, we are expected to insure for virtually everything and anything and at the end of the month there are normally limited funds to insure for the most important issue, YOU.

Do you need it?

Many people feel they do not need life insurance. In some cases this is true but the vast majority have families and feel that they need to be protected in the event of an unexpected death. It is not always the main income provider who needs all the life cover. Provisions must be made if there are children and the non-working parent spends his or her time looking after them. The cost of employing a child minder or even giving up your full time job must be considered. This could be easily remedied with a basic life insurance policy.

If you have a mortgage the banks and building societies normally insist that you have the relevant life insurance to cover the mortgage debt and in the case of endowment mortgages the life insurance forms part of your endowment premiums, but with repayment mortgages the cost of premiums is extra. As you are probably aware, if you haven't got any life cover other than in conjunction with your mortgage then you are likely to be under-insured. If you are in an occupational pension scheme you are likely to have cover as part of your benefits. This would normally work out to be 3 times your basic salary and if you have a personal pension plan you can have life cover up to 3 times and you would receive tax relief on your premiums.

To establish how much life cover you require you need to calculate how much income the family needs to survive each year. Take away any state benefits you would be or are entitled to and then multiply this figure by the number of years your youngest child has before he or she leaves school.

Different types of life insurance

Most forms of life insurance are paid on a monthly or yearly premium basis. The premium you pay will purchase a level of cover and it can be on a fixed or variable term. There are a multitude of insurance policies geared to the individual's needs and requirements, and we will now look at the differences.

Decreasing Term Assurance

This policy is commonly known as mortgage protection and is normally used in conjunction with a repayment mortgage. As we have already discovered with a repayment mortgage the debt reduces further throughout the term and the same can be said about the decreasing term insurance. The amount of life cover will decrease in line with the mortgage. This policy can be written in joint names and is the cheapest form of life assurance available. There is no investment value to this contract and in the event of a claim, the benefits are payable to the estate.

Level term insurance

This policy works on the same basis as the above, but the life cover will not reduce as the term goes on. For this reason, the premiums are slightly more expensive.

Family income benefit policy

This policy will simply provide an annual income for your dependents instead of a lump sum. This is a good way too ensure that the provisions that you have made are not used up in one spending spree. Once again, this contract can be written in joint names, but has no investment value.

Whole life Insurance

This type of policy is considered to be the most flexible contract in the life insurance market. Unlike the other contracts this policy does have investment value and it is not written on a fixed term. The amount of cover you require can be altered at any time to suit changes in your personal circumstances. The premiums you pay are not fixed and are reviewed every 5-10 years to establish whether the insurance cover can still offer you the level of cover for the premium you are paying. This policy is quite expensive in comparison to term policies. It is, however a great deal more flexible and it can be written in joint names.

Critical illness

A new innovation in the insurance industry is the introduction of critical illness insurance.

Surveys have shown that more people are concerned about being diagnosed as having a critical illness than they are of dying. The implications of having a major illness are immense as you could find yourself stuck with the financial commitments but without the income and ability to pay them. The introduction of critical illness means that if you are diagnosed with any of the defined illnesses in the contract, you will receive a lump sum. The amount of the lump sum depends on your premiums and your age. The benefit of critical illness means that you can afford private medical treatment or afford to pay off your debts. Below are listed the main conditions that are considered to be critical illness:

-multiple Sclerosis--heart attack--kidney failure--loss of a limb
-stroke--major organ transplant—cancer—Coma--benign brain tumour
-severe burns

This is not a technical guide or a total list of definitions. It is simply a selection of some definitions. Critical illness can be taken out by itself, or as part of a whole life or endowment. Critical illness does not have investment value. It can be written in joint names.

What the benefits might be
The greater of the sum assured and the encashment value of the plan will be payable on the diagnosis of one of the lives assured suffering a critical illness.

****

Chapter 16

Savings Generally

It is very important indeed to ensure that, as you move towards retirement, or have entered retirement, that you have a firm grasp on your money. Money is not so easy to come by and easy to lose, particularly in the age of the internet and the associated scams.

Maximising your savings

The fact that interest rates have gone down drastically at the time of writing, (2021) means that people are now having to look very carefully at where they save their money in order to get the highest return.

People save for a number of different reasons, dependent on their circumstances and on age. Some people save in order to have enough to help their children and others save for a prosperous old age. Whatever the reason, it is important to understand the best vehicles for savings

Those skilled in the art of financial planning consider that a sum of between three and six months expenditure constitutes an adequate fund for emergencies. This will depend on your employment status as if you are self-employed then you may need more due to the fact that you will not get sick pay unless you are insured.

This emergency cash should be placed in an account that is readily accessible, probably in an instant access account which allows you to withdraw without penalty. However, these accounts traditionally pay the lowest form of interest and it is advisable to shop around.

There are a number of accounts which offer a higher rate of interest with instant access. You are provided with a card so that you can gain access to your money as and when you need it. If the account is joint then both partners should be provided with a card. Although some of the providers are large established institutions, some are smaller companies with far less capital. You should always think before investing with any company. Think about your needs and requirements and the security of your capital. Which? has a comparison site: www.moneycompare.which.co.uk/savings-and-isas/instant-access-savings-accounts-that you may find useful.

Cash returns

A lot of savers like to have more cash on deposit than they need for emergencies. If you do not need access to the money for emergencies then it is better to put your money in a higher rate account, one which generally needs notice of withdrawal. The longer the period of notice the more interest that you will get on your money.

Postal accounts pay higher than standard rates of interest and these are useful for those savers who do not require access to their savings over a foreseeable period. One good website which compares rates on postal accounts is: www.fairinvestment.co.uk/postal_savings_accounts.aspx

You can also get an idea of interest rates by perusing the pages of the dailies and weekend editions of papers, which compare the costs of borrowing and returns on savings. In the United Kingdom rates for deposits are usually quoted gross of tax. The nominal rate is the rate of interest applied to the account, while the annual effective rate (AER) is the rate taking into account the frequency of interest payments.

The nominal rate is not affected by whether you draw your interest or leave it in the account. But if interest is paid more than once a year and you leave it there, you will earn interest on the interest and end the year with more in your account. If you plan to spend all your interest, you can compare different accounts on the basis of their nominal interest rates. If you plan to leave the interest to accumulate, as the table shows, an account with a lower nominal interest rate could give you a better deal if it is credited more frequently. In this case, you should use the annual effective rate as a comparison.

Personal savings allowances

Since April 2016, savers have been able to grow their money tax free, thanks to the 'personal savings allowance.' This allowance allows you to earn interest up to £1,000 interest tax-free if you're a basic-rate (20%) taxpayer, or £500 if you're a higher-rate (40%) taxpayer. Additional-rate taxpayers don't receive a personal savings allowance, so if you earn more than £150,000 each year, you'll need to pay tax on all your savings.

All interest from savings will be paid gross, which means tax will no longer be deducted by your bank or building society. HMRC has provided a few useful examples to illustrate how the allowance works in practice for basic and higher-rate taxpayers: You earn £20,000 a year and get £250 in account interest – you won't pay any tax because it's less than your £1,000 allowance. You earn £20,000 a year and get £1,500 in account interest – you won't pay tax on your interest up to £1,000. But you'll need to pay basic rate tax (20%) on the £500 above this. You earn £60,000 a year and get £250 in account interest – you won't pay any tax because it's less than your £500 allowance. You earn £60,000 a year and get £1,100 in account interest – you won't pay tax on your interest up to £500. But you'll need to pay higher rate tax (40%) on the £600 above this.

Savings income covered by the personal savings allowance
The personal savings allowance applies to interest you earn from any non-Isa savings accounts and current accounts. There are exceptions – namely Isas and some NS&I savings products, such as Premium bonds. These aren't covered by the personal savings allowance, because they are already tax free. The personal savings allowance applies to some investments, too. You can use your personal savings allowance against interest earned from: government or corporate bonds, peer-to-peer lending interest, interest distributions, i.e. income from bond funds, from authorised unit trusts, open-ended investment companies and investment trusts.

In a nutshell, whether your investment income is taxed as savings or as a dividend depends on the underlying investments. Income from loan-based investments, including the above, will be taxed as interest, while profits from equity investments (buying shares in companies) are taxed as dividend income.
Profit from rental properties is taxed in the same way as work or pensions income.

Can interest from savings push me into a higher tax bracket?
Yes, savings income within the allowance still counts towards the basic or higher-rate limits – and may therefore affect the level you're entitled to and the rate of tax due on any excess income. So, if you are a basic-rate taxpayer and you earn enough interest from savings to be pushed into the higher-rate tax threshold,

you are only entitled to a £500 allowance and will pay 40% tax on the remainder. In 2021-22, the higher-rate tax threshold in most of the UK is £50,270. In Scotland, the higher-rate threshold works slightly differently. You pay 41% income tax on income above £43,662 in 2021-22.

Exceed personal savings allowance

In most cases, any tax due will be collected automatically through the pay-as-you-earn (PAYE) system, using information provided by banks and building societies. You should be issued with a 'notice of coding' if this is the case. Or, it can be declared on a self-assessment tax return as normal if you usually complete one. Under long-term plans to transform the current tax system, interest could eventually be processed directly from individual digital tax accounts.

Paying too much tax on interest

You can reclaim tax paid on your savings interest, if your bank or building society didn't make use of your full personal savings allowance. Fill in form R40 to claim the tax you were wrongly charged. You can claim tax on savings from up to four tax years ago. It'll normally take around six weeks to get your money back.

The 'savings starter rate'

In addition to the personal savings allowance, an extra tax break already helps those on a low income pay either no tax or reduced tax on their savings. This £5,000 'starting rate for savings' means anyone with total taxable income under their personal income tax allowance plus £5,000 will not pay any tax on your savings. This means if your total taxable income is less than £17,500 for 2020-21, you won't pay any tax on your savings. It helps to think of these allowances sitting on top of each other; first the personal allowance (£12,570 for 2021-22), then the £5,000 starting savings rate at 0%, and finally the personal savings allowance worth up to £1,000. When HMRC calculates the tax you owe, they'll first look at your income from other sources, and then from your savings income.

Are ISA's worth it?

Even though there are now generous tax breaks on savings, and interest on non-ISA savings accounts tends to be higher, there are still significant long-term benefits to ISA's, particularly if you're a high earner or you have substantial savings. It's likely that the best way to boost returns and minimise tax is to combine a range of savings products and ISA's, as well as high-interest current accounts if you don't mind switching banks.

It's also worth bearing in mind that the personal savings allowance will protect your interest from tax this year – but if you're growing savings over the long term once they're in your ISA they'll be tax free forever. Read below about various scams relating to ISA's

The choice of accounts

There are a wide variety of accounts available from banks and building societies. Many accounts have differing features. Most pay variable interest but some pay fixed rates. The following are some of the accounts on offer.

Children's accounts

These accounts sometimes offer better variable rates than can be gained on a small deposit on a regular savings account. These accounts can also offer free gifts for children, such as magazines, moneyboxes etc. A good website which will give you an idea of the entire range of savings accounts available to children, such as Child trust Funds, Junior ISA's etc is www.deal-review.co.uk. Another useful site is www.moneysavingexpert.com

Instant access accounts

These permit withdrawal of capital without notice, though there is usually a restriction on how much cash can be withdrawn on one day. The interest rate is variable. Interest may be credited yearly, half yearly, quarterly, monthly or daily. With most accounts, the rate will depend on the amount invested. You can get a good idea of the various savings accounts by accessing the numerous comparison sites or by looking at the weekend papers, such as the Times, Telegraph, Guardian etc.

Individual Savings Accounts (ISA's)

There are numerous ISA's on the market. The mainstream ISA allows you to invest up to £20,000 per annum in either a cash ISA or a stocks and shares ISA or a mixture of the two. In addition, there is a new lifetime ISA (LISA), launched from April 2017, which can be taken out by those between 18-40 and which is designed to help people to save for the longer term, and can help to boost pension savings. Up to £4,000 per year can be saved in a LISA and the state will boost this with an annual bonus of 25%. the bonus is paid until you hit 50. The bonus is paid annually in the 2021/2022 tax year and then monthly in the following tax years. The bonus is paid on contributions and the maximum bonus you can get is £32,000.

Innovative finance ISAs

These include:

- peer-to-peer loans - loans that you give to other people or businesses without using a bank
- 'crowdfunding debentures' - investing in a business by buying its debt

You cannot transfer any peer-to-peer loans you've already made or crowdfunding debentures you already hold into an innovative finance ISA. One very good site for ISA rates is www.top-isa-rates.co.uk.

Children's ISA's (JISA) have a savings limit of £9,000 from April 2021/22. They remain tax-fee up until 18yrs old and can provide good vehicles to build up a lump sum for the future. www.moneysavingexpert.com/savings/junior-isa is a good site to explore for information regarding children's ISA's. In addition, there are numerous other sites.

For more comprehensive information on all aspects of ISA's you should go to the .Gov site www.gov.uk/individual-savings-accounts

A note of caution generally with ISA's
Watch out – Online scammers

The internet is awash with bogus Isa providers trying to persuade you to part with your cash – and the run-up to the end of the tax year is likely to be a time when scammers ramp up their efforts.

Dozens of scam websites are offering eye-catching rates, sometimes touting returns in double figures, and they often appear at the top of Google searches for terms such as "top Isa rates" and "protected savings" .The also use words such as "secure", "safe" and "low-risk" to convince savers their money will be protected. Some use logos of official bodies that do not back them, as well as falsely claiming association with reputable organisations such as Trustpilot and national newspapers.

The Sunday Times and campaigners have reported more than 100 suspicious-looking websites to the City regulator, the Financial Conduct Authority (FCA). Many have paid Google for prominence and appear with an "Ad" logo next to them. Although Google will eliminate a scam website from its search results when informed, many change their names or internet address and then reappear. Google says that it has robust systems in place to monitor scam sites and remove companies that do not comply with its rules. The FCA and big insurers have called for tougher legislation to force Google to take them down.

The government says that the FCA already has strong powers to tackle the problem. While scammers can continue taking advantage of laws to advertise their schemes, it is important to be on your guard against bogus deals.

How to spot a scam ISA site
Scam websites will typically advertise rates that are much higher than those available on the high street or via well known comparison websites such as Moneyfacts and Moneysupermarket. For example, some have offered annual returns as high as 30 per cent. The most you can hope to get from a well-known brand is about 2per cent. The websites may also deliberately conflate different types of Isa: for example, regular Isas and innovative finance ISA. The latter invest in loans and are not protected by the Financial Services Compensation Scheme (FSCS), the government safety net to protect savers in case anything goes wrong. Most will not have a company number, address or telephone contact number. No respectable organisation offering financial services would leave out such

details. Instead, savers are invited to enter an email address or telephone number, after which they will receive emails from high-risk or fraudulent firms. The websites effectively act as unregulated introducers to these dodgy providers. Should you be contacted, the caller may say they can offer you a rare opportunity to save in something that has guaranteed returns. They may also tell you there is only a narrow window of opportunity, to pressure you into investing. Never be Pressured. You may be sent authentic-looking documents by email that will, without permission, use the branding of well-known firms such as AXA, Blackrock or Barclays. Do not be taken in. Some of the websites will provide an address in a high-end postcode. This will also often claim to be protected by the FSCS. Use its website to check, fscs.org.uk If you see a great deal, check the FCA's fraud warning list to see if the watchdog believes that it is a scam, and do some research to confirm that a company has the professional backing it claims to have. You can check the FCA's register to see if a firm is authorised. If it is, use the contact details that the company gives you, to avoid being duped by fraudulent "clone" of a genuine organisation. Many promotions appear to break rules stating that only regulated financial firms can promote investments – an offence punishable by up to two years in prison.

Monthly income accounts

These types of accounts may have a minimum notice period for withdrawal. The income is usually paid direct to your current account and there is usually a £250 minimum amount. www.thisismoney.co.uk shows a good range of monthly income accounts.

Notice accounts

Money can be withdrawn without penalty by giving the appropriate amount of notice. If you withdraw without notice you will lose interest on the amount you would have been paid during the notice period. There is usually a minimum deposit of £1000 or more. there are numerous websites giving details of notice accounts and also the weekend supplements in the main newspapers also provide information.

Time deposits

The interest rate is fixed for the time of the deposit, often 30 days onwards. There will be a penalty for early withdrawal. Interest is usually added at the end of the period that is fixed and is usually gross of tax.

Fixed-rate investments

You can commit your money for a fixed period; say five years, at a certain rate of interest, say 3%. If rates are at 0.5% this may seem attractive but rates can rise during the period. Before investing for the longer term at fixed rates you should consider carefully the market in the longer term and decide whether you want to make this gamble. Fixed interest rates will offer you a reasonable return over the period and it is difficult to predict interest rates over the longer term. Again, the main websites, such as this ismoney will provide comparisons, as will the financial pages of the main newspapers.

Short-term fixed-rate investments-Escalator bonds

These are issued by building societies and pay a rate of interest that rises each year for a fixed period. Since these are fixed rate accounts you cannot get it back early or there can be a significant financial penalty.

You should always think about the consequences of your wish to invest in this type of product.

Fixed rate bonds

These accounts pay a flat fixed rate of interest for a fixed period from one to five years. Early withdrawal is not usually permitted without a penalty. There will be a minimum investment.

Guaranteed growth bonds

Issued by insurance companies, these guarantee a fixed rate for a specified period, usually between two and five years. A lump sum is paid at the end of the term. The return is treated as having borne basic rate tax so there will only be an additional liability if you are a higher rate taxpayer.

Guaranteed income bonds

These pay a fixed income for a specified term, usually two to five years. The tax treatment is the same as for the above bonds.

National Savings Certificates

These grow in value at a fixed rate for a period of up to five years. The profits are exempt from tax and there are limits on how much you can invest.

National Savings Pensioners Guaranteed Bonds

These pay a fixed amount of income over two to five years. The interest is taxable but is paid without deduction at source.

Unit trust savings plans

Unit trusts and open-ended investment companies are similar in having a pool of money which they manage on behalf of individual and corporate investors. The pool expands or contracts depending on the additions or withdrawals into it and the value of a unit or share is the value of the investments in the pool divided by the number of units or shares in issue. A wide variety of funds are available, investing in a variety of areas and countries. Minimum monthly savings are from £30-£50. The income received is taxable and will usually be taxed at source. Higher rate taxpayers will receive a certificate showing what they have paid at source and they will be personally responsible for any extra payments. Costs vary from 1%-5% of each contribution with an annual charge of 0.5% to 2% of the value of your assets. You can take out a plan in the name of a child.

Investment trusts
Unlike unit trusts or open-ended investment companies, investment trusts do not issue new shares to savers but buy existing shares through the stock market. This is because investment trusts have a fixed pool of assets and the price of a share in the market may be higher or lower than its net asset value. These schemes are run by investment trust managers. They usually subsidise the costs of the plan, which are much lower than the costs of buying investment trust shares through a stockbroker. The annual charges are between 0.5% and 2%. The taxation rules and child rules are the same as for unit trusts.

With profits savings plans
With profits savings plans are in the form of endowment polices issued by insurance companies. Though they are life policies, they provide very little life cover. Most of the premiums that are paid are used to invest in the companies with profits fund, which is a giant pool of assets usually worth billions of pounds. The

fund will hold a variety of assets including fixed rate investments, UK and overseas shares and property.

The with-profits policy has a sum assured, which is the minimum amount that is paid on death or at the maturity rate. Two types of bonus are added to the sum assured. Reversionary bonuses are added each year, often at quite a lower rate of 3% or so. At maturity (or death) a terminal bonus is added which can be equal to al the reversionary bonuses paid. Once a reversionary bonus has been added to a policy, it cannot be taken away, but terminal bonus rates are not guaranteed and can be varied at any time.

With-profits policies are of two types. Some have one fixed maturity date, while with a 'flexible policy' you can en-cash it at several different dates, usually at five-year intervals. The charges for with profits policies are typically about 12-15% of premiums over the term. The term for these policies is usually quite long, being anything from 10-25 years so careful thought needs to be given to this type of investment. They are only really suitable if you can sustain your savings over this long period.

Friendly society plans

Friendly societies are permitted to run tax-free savings schemes with low minimum and maximum investments. Some are of the with-profit types, while others are unit-linked. The plans have a minimum term of ten years and the high costs can wipe out other benefits so again careful thought has to be given to this type of investment.

The purpose of saving

The purposes of saving, as we have seen, are many and will differ, depending on your circumstances and long-term view.

Some of the more usual savings objectives are to provide retirement income, to pay for children's education, to reduce debt such as mortgage and for general purposes, for life's little luxuries. Whatever you choose you should do so carefully, think about the short and long-term advantages and don't take unnecessary risks.

Other savings schemes-peer-to-peer lending

Peer to peer lending is for those who wish to take a gamble with their savings in order to obtain a better rate of return than that offered by mainstream banks.

What is peer-to-peer?

Peer-to-peer lending enables individuals to lend to each other, bypassing the need for a traditional bank or building society. Money from individual lenders is put together to fund borrowers seeking personal or small business loans and in some cases, buy-to-let mortgages. Lending in the sector reached 6billion by the end of June 2017, according to the peer-to-peer finance association. Platforms such as Zoopla and Ratesetter display rates based on how long your money is locked up for and how risky a borrower is deemed to be by the platform.

As with the savings market, the longer your money is tied up for the better the rate of return. The products work like a normal savings product, paying interest monthly or quarterly but accessing your funds can be more difficult because the process relies on another lender wanting to buy and there may be an access fee. You can earn your interest tax free using the Innovative Tax-Free ISA. At the time of writing many platforms are waiting approval from the Financial Conduct Authority for ISA manager status.

Peer-to-peer loans do not benefit from the Financial Services Compensation Scheme, which protects up to £85,000 of savings, but if you invest via a financial advisor you benefit from £85,000 protection.

Investing a Lump Sum

If you are able to consider investing a lump sum of money, you must take great care in establishing your requirements for that investment and also your own future plans.

For example:

- you may not be worried about getting a significant return as long as it is likely to better the return you would get from your building society account;
- you need the best return possible over the next five years without jeopardizing capital;
- you aren't worried how the money is invested provided you don't receive a tax bill;

Quite clearly, the important issues to remember when investing a lump sum are:

1. the amount of money you can afford to invest;
2. the term of the investment;
3. the risk involved with the investment;
4. tax implications.

As we have already seen, there are numerous ways in which you can invest your money and the same considerations should be made whether you are saving on a regular basis or a lump sum.

The options available

Your choice of investment will obviously depend on your own personal financial circumstances. Below you will find details of the most popular investments currently available.

Higher interest building society accounts

If you are concerned about the risk attached with investing your money, then you cannot do a lot better than your building society. Although some people may consider investing in their building society as unattractive, with rates now at the time of writing at an all time low, you haven't got any worries about how your money is being invested. For lump sums, building societies often offer a wide range of higher rate accounts with a tiered rate of interest, depending on the size of investment. Most higher rate accounts have a notice period which must be given for any withdrawals. This may not apply, however, if the balance of the account remains over £5,000. A large number of higher rate accounts will allow you to take a regular income on a monthly basis. Remember, from April 2016, the first £1000 of interest received from savings is tax fee. A good site comparing building society accounts is www.money.co.uk/savings-accounts.htm

Ordinary accounts

This is a basic account which will allow you to invest between £10-£10,000.

Index linked Savings certificates

This is a good way of investing your money over a five-year period especially if interest rates are high. The interest you will receive is fixed and tax-free. For more details about this type of investment go to www.nsandi.com.

Investment bonds

Investment bonds are considered a medium to long-term investment and the investment options range from the with profits investments to investments in the property markets and overseas. The risk is always a major factor in any investment and you should be aware exactly where your money is being invested and the relative risk.

All major insurance companies offer investment bonds and they can be used for both capital growth and income if required. The investment fund is taxable and payments are made net of basic rate tax. There is an allowance however, which will allow both basic rate and higher rate taxpayers to withdraw up to 5% of the fund value each year without liability.

The minimum amount that you can invest in a bond is normally £2,000 and you should consider investing it for a minimum of five years. In the case of an emergency, you would be able to gain access to your money but the value will relate to the period of investment, charges and market conditions.

The main points to remember are that you should invest in a bond that suits your attitude to risk. If you are a higher rate taxpayer you may be able to reduce any liability if you can cash in the bond when the income drops to the basic rate bracket.

Guaranteed Capital Investments

This is a relatively new concept in the insurance industry as your investment is directly linked to the performance of the FTSE one hundred. If you read the financial press or watch the main television news you will always see a reference to the FTSE one hundred. It provides a clear indication of how the stock market is behaving as it monitors the share prices of the top 100 companies in the UK.

From day to day the prices of each company's shares can change for any reason and towards the bottom of the index the smaller companies are constantly competing to secure their position within the top 100.

The growth of the FTSE is often compared to that of banks and building societies (see single premium investments) and over a long term period is considered to be a valuable alternative to the standard options. Traditionally, the FTSE has outperformed the returns offered by building society accounts and for that reason most insurance companies will guarantee that on completion of the five year term you will at least receive your original investment, thereby reducing the risk factor.

The minimum investment is usually £6,000 and the fund and benefits are paid net of basic rate tax. Guaranteed capital investments are offered on limited availability and are not able to provide an income. They are, however, a worthwhile consideration when you are building up an investment portfolio..

A good website here is www.bestinvestor.co.uk/Guaranteed_Capital_Funds although at the time of writing (October 2020) the website is undergoing a refreshment. there are numerous other websites, such as Hargreaves Lansdowne https://www.hl.co.uk/Buy-Funds/Online

Unit Trusts

The purpose of the unit trust is to give individuals the opportunity to invest directly in the stock market. There are a multitude of investment opportunities ranging from UK equities to shares in Japan and North America. In order to overcome the charges and realise a profit, you must look at investing your money in a unit trust for at least three years or longer.

Unit trusts can be used for capital growth or income and you should obtain help from a financial advisor to choose the most suitable trust for your performance. Once you have chosen your trust and paid your money, you will be issued with a certificate. It is very important that you keep this in a safe place as you will need to produce it when you cash it in.

To establish how well your investment is doing, you can phone the trust managers or look at the share page of any quality newspaper. You will normally see two columns, the offer price and the bid price. For the purpose of selling you must multiply the bid price by the number of units you hold. A good site for more information about unit trusts is www.money.co.uk

The tax implications
Unless you are a higher rate tax-payer it is unlikely that you will have any tax liability on the income or gain of the investment. If you are a higher rate tax-payer there are various ways of mitigating your liability and you should discuss this with a financial advisor before committing yourself to any investment.

A quick word about crypto currencies
In the last few years, cryptocurrencies such as bitcoin, and now a host of other currencies have come to the fore and quite a few people in the know have invested in them. However, it is the case that most people don't understand them and wouldn't go near them. Not surprising, as there are an awful lot of scams out there. Below is a brief outline of crypto-currencies.

What is a cryptocurrency?
Bitcoin was the first cryptocurrency, and is still the biggest, but in the twelve years since it was first used pretenders to the

throne have come along. All of them have the same basic underpinnings: they use a "blockchain", a shared public record of transactions, to create and track a new type of digital token – one that can only be made and shared according to the agreed-upon rules of the network, whatever they may be. Some cryptocurrencies, such as Litecoin or Dogecoin, fulfil the same purpose as bitcoin – building a new digital currency – with tweaks to some of the details (making transactions faster, for instance, or ensuring a basic level of inflation). Others, such as Ethereum or Bat, take the same principle but apply it to a specific purpose: cloud computing or digital advertising in the case of those two.

What exactly is a bitcoin? Can I hold one?

A bitcoin, or any other cryptocurrency for that matter, doesn't really exist as a concrete physical – or even digital – object. If I have 0.5 bitcoins sitting in my digital wallet, that doesn't mean there is a corresponding other half sitting somewhere else.

What you really have when you own a bitcoin is the collective agreement of every other computer on the bitcoin network that your bitcoin was legitimately created by a bitcoin "miner", and then passed on to you through a series of legitimate transactions.

If you want to actually own some bitcoin, there are two options: either become a miner (which involves investing a lot of money in computers and electricity bills – probably more than the value of the bitcoin you'll actually make, unless you're very smart), or simply buy some bitcoin from someone else using conventional money, typically through a legitimate bitcoin exchange such as Coinbase, Bitfinex., Kraken and Binance.

What can I actually do with cryptocurrencies?

Bitcoin can be used as a payment system for a few online transactions, and now increasingly for other transactions such as some property purchases.

As I stated above, although it is good to understand what all the fuss is about, investing in bitcoin and other cryptocurrencies is not for the fain hearted and is not recommended unless you have a firm grasp of the nature of the beast! The idea is to make quick returns, or higher returns than can be made elsewhere. There are numerous websites recommending that you invest in bitcoin, avoid them unless you are sure of what you are doing. In fact, TSB has become the first bank to ban cryptocurrency as fraud escalates and scammers are cloning legitimate sites.

Savings APPS

Automated savings plans are offered by money apps that use algorithms to analyse your spending habits. Savings apps such as Chips, Tandem, Moneybox and Plum work out how much money you can afford to squirrel away – and make the transfer on your behalf. Plum analyses your daily spend and transfers small amounts into a savings account about five times a month. You can choose between six settings to guide the app on how much to save. It is a good way to get into savings habit, although some app accounts do not pay the best interest rates. Plum's easy access account, for example, pays just 0.6 per cent. Some pay nothing at all. You can authorise the robots behind some of the apps to round up the spare change from your debits card transactions and stash away the difference. For instance, if your coffee costs £2.00, 80p is automatically transferred to a nominated savings account. Some of the high street banks are on board too, Lloyds Banking Group (Lloyds, Halifax and Bank of

Scotland) offers a similar Save the Change service. Nationwide customers can do the same using its Impulse Saver. If it is better rates you are looking for, the cash savings platform Octopus Cash, Raisin, Flagstone and Hargreaves Lansdown Active Savings give you automatic access to a range of accounts with banks. Once registered with Octopus Cash, for example, you can switch between seven partner banks, which means you do not need to spend time filling in forms to open an account with a new company; You can do it with a few clicks online. These platforms are typically for large cash savings.

****

Chapter 17

Financing Funeral Plans

Financing Funerals

Funeral Plans

Funeral plans and over 50s plans are two different ways of paying for part of a funeral in advance. Here's what to bear in mind if you're thinking about taking one out.

Why use a funeral plan?

Many people worry that when they die, they won't leave enough money for their funeral and their loved ones will be left with the bill. With a funeral plan, you arrange and pay for it in advance, so your relatives don't have to cover all the cost themselves. You can arrange a funeral plan for your own funeral or for someone else's, as long as it's held in the UK.

With a standard funeral plan, you pay for your funeral in advance, at today's prices. You can pay the plan provider in either a lump sum or installments. You can buy a plan from most funeral directors.

Funeral plans vary in terms of what's included. All plans include the services of a funeral director who takes care of the deceased, arranges the funeral and organises transport. However, there are differences with the additional services that plans offer. Some may provide high-quality coffins, access to view the deceased in a chapel of rest, and limousines to transport guests to the funeral. Other plans may be more basic.

As well as the core costs of the funeral director and coffin, funeral plans will also include – or make a provision for – third-party costs. These can include the cost of using a crematorium, doctors' fees and the cost of a minister or celebrant. These third-party costs are usually called 'disbursements'.

If you're buying a cremation funeral plan, it won't usually cover the cost of disbursements in full. Instead, they're covered by an allowance, which rises in line with inflation. However, there's a risk that if funeral costs rise faster than inflation, there won't be quite enough money in your plan to cover these costs. This would leave your family or estate with extra to pay when you die. Some funeral plans offer a guarantee to cover all third-party costs.

If you're opting for a burial funeral plan, it will usually include the cost of digging the grave. But the cost of the burial plot – as well as extras such as headstones – won't be included. Funeral plans never include the cost of flowers or organising a wake. But some plans allow you to put aside some extra money to cover these costs.

It's important to make sure you know what your plan does and doesn't provide before you pay.

How safe is money in a funeral plan?

Your money must either be invested in a trust fund with trustees, or in an insurance policy, which is then used to pay for the funeral.Funeral plans aren't currently regulated. But the government has announced plans to bring them under regulation by the Financial Conduct Authority.

For now, the industry relies on a voluntary regulator called the Funeral Planning Authority (FPA). They don't offer the same level of protection for customers as a government regulator, but they do have a set of standards their members have to follow. They also help to resolve customer complaints. Make sure that you only buy plans from companies that are part of the FPA. You can check their list of members on the FPA website.

If you're paying for your funeral plan in a lump sum, you could consider paying for part of it on your credit card. When you pay with your credit card, you can get extra protection if things go wrong with the funeral director. You could also get this protection if you were to pay at least £100 on your credit card, and then pay the rest in installments. If you die before you've finished paying the installments, your family or estate will need to pay the balance. Some plans offer to pay the remaining installments through a form of insurance.

Pros and cons of funeral plans

Pros:

Funeral plans give you the chance to make the arrangements that you want for your funeral. They protect you against rising costs.

Cons:

They can be expensive. Even if you're paying in installments, they're likely to cost at least £20 a month – and often considerably more. If funeral prices fall, you could end up overpaying for your funeral. Some plans don't guarantee all the costs. Funeral plans aren't currently regulated.

Questions to ask the plan provider

- Are there any cancellation charges?
- What exactly is included in the plan and what potential costs are not?

o Could there be any other expenses for the funeral, and what happens if there are?

o Is it possible to cancel the plan if circumstances change, for example if you've arranged for your spouse's funeral but you later separate?

o Does the plan allow you to choose the funeral director?

o What if your chosen funeral director goes out of business?

o What happens if the person the funeral is intended for dies abroad or away from home?

o Can the funeral director arrange a funeral of a different standard from the one you've chosen?

o If you pay by installments, how long do you do this for and do you have to pay interest?

o What happens if there are outstanding installments at death?

o What freedom do you have to change the details of your funeral plan?

o How does the funeral planning company know about the plan holder's death?

Over 50s plans

Over 50s plans are insurance policies that guarantee to pay out when you die. You pay a fixed amount every month for the rest of your life. In most cases, the payout doesn't rise with inflation. They can be poor value if you live a long life – as you'll end up paying in much more than you'll get out.

However, they may be right for you if you can't afford a funeral plan and you don't trust yourself to save for your funeral in a savings account, without spending the money on something else.

Pros and cons of over 50s plans

Pros:

Over 50s plans don't need any medical underwriting. This means that being in poor health makes no difference to your payout. You can pay as much as you can afford – unlike funeral plans where minimum premiums are much higher.

Cons:

In most cases, you lose your whole payout, and you won't get any money back, if you stop paying in the first few years. However, some providers are now offering payment holidays to give you some breathing space if you're struggling to keep up with payments. And a growing number of policies will still protect some of your payout if you stop paying after a certain number of years. The payout on most plans doesn't increase with inflation. This means many people end up paying more in premiums than their payout. Whole of Life insurance could pay out more than 40% more when you die than an over 50s plan – according to Which?. You usually need to survive beyond the first two years of an over 50s plan to get the full payout.

Some plans require you to continue paying premiums until you die. This means that if you live a very long time, you could pay far more in premiums than you'll get back.

If you do decide to take out a funeral plan or over 50s plan, keep the paperwork in a safe place and make sure your next of kin know about it.

Alternatives to funeral plans and over 50s plans
Putting money into a savings account

Putting a little money aside each month is one straightforward way to save for a funeral. This isn't risk-free though, as you may die before you build up enough to pay for a funeral. And many people worry that they may not have the discipline to leave their savings untouched.

Using the money you leave behind in your will

You may have assets that can be sold when you die, such as your house. You could make it clear in your will that you want these to be used to pay for your funeral. However, it can take some time for properties to be sold after someone dies. So it's worth talking to the family member who you want to arrange your funeral and checking that they have enough to pay upfront.

Death in service from an employer

Some employers provide a payout if you die while you're still working for them. If you're a member of a trade union, professional body or other association, they might pay a benefit when a member dies. Contact them to find out.

Life insurance

Using the lump sum payment from a life insurance policy can pay for a funeral. According to the Association of British Insurers, payments are generally made about a month after the policyholder dies. It could be longer if the death needs to be investigated.

More information about funerals

The sources of information differ depending on where you live:

For England and Wales, visit GOV.UK
For Northern Ireland, visit nidirect
For Scotland, visit www.mygov.scot

In addition, Ageuk offer useful advice on planning for funerals www.ageuk.org.uk

****

Chapter 18

Investing in Stocks and Shares

The stock market generally

It is true to say that, for many years, the ownership of stocks and shares and the workings of the stock exchange were a mystery to most people. Shares and the stock exchange were seen to be a specialist areas dominated by the well heeled and, invariably, the old-school tie network. Times have changed and now share ownership is within everyone's grasp. This has been so because of changes in the ownership of former public utilities and the dispersing of shares to the ordinary person. Alongside that has come an opening up of the whole area of share dealing.

However, over the last few years we have seen some horror stories about the stock market and investors losing a lot of money. Some of these losses have been in mini-bond investments, i.e. the Woodford Funds and also London Capital and Finance and also in assorted other investments. This emphasises the fact that investing in stocks and shares can be very risky indeed and, rather than make money you can also lose money.

BREXIT, COVID 19 and the stock market

Over the last two years in the UK, 2020-2021, no two events have had a greater impact on stock market indices, including the FTSE 100, than Brexit and Covid -19. The FTSE 100 has either risen or fallen with almost every new Brexit and Covid-19 development as investors have speculated on what each one could mean for the economy and, most importantly, for their investments.

BREXIT

Stock market indices like the FTSE 100 have shown significant sensitivity to Brexit news and headlines ever since the shock 2016 referendum result. On 24 June 2016, the day that the referendum results were announced, the FTSE 100 fell by 9%. Since then, other Brexit developments have been accompanied by swings in the FTSE 100 and other stock market indices.

Short term investment trends-making a quick buck

Another area that has grown is that of the speculative investor looking for quick returns. Unless you really know what you are doing, then it pays to keep in mind that you are an investor and therefore should look carefully and spot those industries that will likely grow in the future and invest for the medium to ling term, balancing your portfolio to achieve that aim. An example of short-term speculative investing is what happened recently in the case of Gamestop.

In early January, Gamestop was looking like a company about to go the way of Blockbuster Video. A fixture in most suburban shopping malls in the US, it is a chain of 5,000 shops, headquartered in Texas, selling games, consoles and other electronics. The company was in trouble as the shift of video-game sales went online. In 2019, it made a loss of $795 million (around £600 million). Fast-forward to the end of January, when a forum on the social media site Reddit called WallstreetBets – a place where people discussed investing and stocks and shares (and swore a lot) - the 8.5 million members call themselves "the degenerates")–featured an increasing number of posts about

GameStop. The degenerates hatched a plan to teach the hedge fund managers, who were betting that GameStop's value would go down and therefore adding to the likelihood of it collapsing. The hedge fund managers' bets were in the form of "shorting" its stock. This is done by borrowing GameStop's shares and selling them with a promise to buy them back later. If the company you are shorting loses value, you make money when you buy them back at a cheaper price.

The armchair investors took on Wall Street by buying shares in GameStop and encouraging everyone on the forum to do the same, pushing up the value. At one point last year GameStop's shares cost just $2.80; by January 27 this year, they had rocketed to $347,51. One of the loudest voices behind the campaign was Keith Gill, 34, aka "DeepF***ing Value" on Reddit. Until recently, Gill worked for an insurance company in Massachusetts. At the peak of the GameStop frenzy his investment account was worth $48 million.

Get rich quick

So, the above is one way to approach the stock market, if you have the knowledge. In most cases, the stock market is not generally a get rich quick scheme. It is a place to grow expertise, think in the long term and use your good judgment. As mentioned, try to visualise the future performance of companies, for example, a small investment in Amazon and Tesla pre-pandemic will have quadrupled, Amazon in particular.

Ethical Investing

Ethical investing is when individual investors choose the assets and stocks, they will invest in based on their own ethical values and beliefs. This can range from excluding specific firms that operate in areas such as gambling, tobacco, adult entertainment, weapons or alcohol or by selecting funds that the consider a range of ethical factors and/or delivers positive ethical outcomes. Positive ethical outcomes can include social and environmental benefits.

How to invest ethically

Investors can choose their own investments, selecting stock in individual firms based on analysis of their ethical credentials. However, this is time consuming and requires regular research to help make sure your choices remain relevant and offer a good return. A suitable investment fund includes a range of ethical investments based on a set of guiding principles or rules for managing the fund.

Investors can use an investment platform to choose, invest in and manage their ethical investments. One such platform is Tribe Impact Capital, a wealth management firm that offers investments in companies that work towards achieving the United Nations Sustainable Development Goals.

https://tribeimpactcapital.com

Why invest ethically?

Making a choice to invest ethically is not only good for wider society and the environment but ethical investments have been shown to outperform the returns of their non-ethical equivalents. In July 2020 Moneyfacts revealed that 140 ethical unit trusts had grown by 4% in the 12-months to 1 July 2020 compared to a contraction of 1.5% for those not in the ethical category. For very good advice on ethical investing and recommendations of the best ethical investment funds go to:

moneyfacts.co.uk/investments-how-to-invest-your-money/guides/ethical-investing.

Taking into account the numerous perils for the novice investor, this book is intended for anyone who wishes to understand more about the workings of the stock market and also the whole culture and environment of shares and share dealings before diving in.

Knowledge is the key to everything and it is the intention of this book to provide a comprehensive overview of how the stock market works, how companies work, how to go about buying and selling shares and also how to understand information relating to share performance. By discussing the nature of investments, the operations of companies, the stock market, the nature and costs of shares and also the interpretation of data in financial pages, this brief introduction to the stock market should provide enough information for the smaller investor to operate with confidence and to make informed decisions.

By investing carefully, taking time to analyse markets and regularly reading financial data, there is no reason why the small investor cannot prosper on the stock market.

Vehicles for Buying Shares and The Costs of Investing

When considering the initial amount to invest in a parcel of shares, it is important to realise that the less you invest the higher the overall cost of shares, because of fees etc, and the more a share has to rise to make a decent return. It is for this reason that most people in an advisory capacity would say that £2,000 is the minimum that should be invested.

For safety the investment should be spread over a number of companies. The old adage 'don't put all of your eggs in one basket' rings very true here. A common portfolio for a small investor should contain at least 12 companies (but not more as the other factor is that the investor should stay in control of his or her investments). The main aim of all investing is to get a decent return with the minimum acceptable risk. If you own shares in one company then the risk and possibility of losing your money is greater than if the risk is spread.

It is a general rule that the lower the risk the lower the return. However, the converse holds true, the higher the risk the higher the return. For some people who invest in a single company the rewards can be big if the company does well. In truth what usually happens is that large investments in one company will not produce massive returns or result in loss of all ones investment. The shares will usually carry on rising marginally in the longer term.

Buying through Investments Trusts-Purchasing unit trusts

There are benefits connected to the purchase of unit trusts and investment trusts as opposed to individual shares. With trusts you get a spread of investments over a number of companies, cutting the danger of one of the companies going out of business.

Investment trusts

Investment trusts are companies which invest in other companies on behalf of investors. They are termed close-end funds because the number of shares on issue is fixed and does not fluctuate no matter how popular the fund may be. This sort of investment is convenient for small investors who do not have enough money to buy a lot of shares in different companies thereby spreading the risk. An investment trust will have its money spread across a lot of companies so problems with one company will usually be compensated by a boom in another company. Managers of investment trusts are professionals, so, at least in theory, they will do better than the average person. It is true to say that investment companies are as good as their managers so it is wise to pick a company with a good and known track record.

Most investment funds have a lot of money to invest and they will usually invest in blue chip shares, unless specifically set up to invest in a specific type of share. The cost of the stockbroker is the same as it would be with other dealings and the government stamp duty and the price spread between buying and selling price remains the same.

Although investment trust managers do have a lot of say in the nature and type of investments, investors will also have some say in what goes on by buying the right investment trust shares. There are trusts specializing in the higher risk stock markets (called emerging markets); there are some investing in the Pacific Rim and some concentrating in Japan; some go for small companies and some specialize in Europe and the United States and so on. The spread of investments can be very diverse indeed and managers of investment trusts tend to be more adventurous on the whole than managers of unit trusts.

Some trusts are split capital trusts which have a finite life during which one class of share gets all the income, and when it is wound up the other class of share gets the proceeds from selling off the holdings.

Trusts are quoted on the Stock Exchange so the share price can be tracked and also the asset value of the trust can be calculated. The asset value is comprised of the value of the shares that the trust is holding compared with the trusts own share price.

One main reason that many are priced differently than their real value is that major investing institutions avoid trusts. Huge pension funds or insurance companies do not have to buy in to investment expertise as they normally have their own experts. Therefore trusts are used mainly by private investors.

Unit trusts

Unit trusts have the same advantage of spreading risk over a large number of companies and of having the portfolio of shares managed by professionals. However, instead of the units being quoted on the stock market as investment trusts are, investors deal directly with the management company. Therefore the paper issued has no secondary market. The investor cannot sell to anyone other than back to the management company. The market is seen from the manager's viewpoint: it sells units at the offer price and buys them back at the lower 'bid' price, to give it a profit from the spread as well as the management charge. Many unit trust prices are published in quality papers.

These are called 'open-ended' funds, because they are the pooled resources of all investors. If more people want to get into a unit trust it will issue more paper to accommodate them. Unlike the price of investment trust shares, which is set by market demand and can get totally out of line with the market value the price of units is set strictly by the value of shares the trust owns.

Tracker funds

Tracker funds move with the main stock market index, in the U.K that is usually taken to be the FTSE 100. This type of fund is for the less adventurous investor who looks for a virtually risk free return.

Open-ended investment companies

Open Ended Investment companies or OEICs are placed midway between investment trusts and unit trusts. They are incorporated companies and issue shares, like investment companies. Like unit trusts the number of shares on issue depends on how much money investors want to put into the fund. When money is taken out and shares sold back, those shares are cancelled. The companies usually contain a number of shares segmented by specialism. This enables investors to pick the area they prefer and to switch from one fund to another with a minimum of administration and cost.

Advantages of pooled investments

Pooled investments reduce risk and are therefore a safer home for small investors. However, as they are safe they are unlikely to hit the outside chance of a high performer, as individual share speculators might.

As stated earlier, there are many different companies and a certain degree of research and knowledge is essential before committing. To be forewarned is to be forearmed. Quality newspapers will have regular league tables of performance. Be careful too with tables that are published showing performance. Obviously, tables can only look backwards to demonstrate past performance and it is the future that matters.

Trusts can do very well, but it may be that they have done well in a sector that has expanded and is now contracting.

Management charges for both investment trusts and unit trusts are usually high. One way of avoiding high charges is to opt for a U.S. mutual fund, which is the same as a unit trust and which has lower charges.

There is also the alternative of setting up your own investment vehicle which has become quite popular over the years. Investment clubs, described below, already very popular in the United States are growing more popular up in the U.K. Basically, a group of people together pool cash for investment in the stock market. The usual way is for each member to set aside a regular amount each month and decide where to invest it. This has the advantages of avoiding charges, spreading investments and also the social spin off. Also, the work of researching shares is spread amongst members.

Exchange traded funds

Exchange-traded funds, or ETFs, are investment companies that are legally classified as open-end companies or Unit Investment Trusts (UITs), but that differ from traditional open-end companies and UITs in the following respects:

- ETFs do not sell individual shares directly to investors and only issue their shares in large blocks (blocks of 50,000 shares, for example) that are known as "Creation Units."
- Investors generally do not purchase Creation Units with cash. Instead, they buy Creation Units with a basket of securities that generally mirrors the ETF's portfolio. Those who purchase Creation Units are frequently institutions.
- After purchasing a Creation Unit, an investor often splits it up and sells the individual shares on a secondary market. This permits other investors to purchase individual shares (instead of Creation Units).

Investors who want to sell their ETF shares have two options: (1) they can sell individual shares to other investors on the secondary market, or (2) they can sell the Creation Units back to the ETF. In addition, ETFs generally redeem Creation Units by

184

giving investors the securities that comprise the portfolio instead of cash. So, for example, an ETF invested in the stocks contained in the Dow Jones Industrial Average (DJIA) would give a redeeming shareholder the actual securities that constitute the DJIA instead of cash. Because of the limited redeemability of ETF shares, ETFs are not considered to be—and may not call themselves—mutual funds.

An ETF, like any other type of investment company, will have a prospectus. All investors that purchase Creation Units receive a prospectus. Some ETFs may furnish an investor with a summary prospectus containing key information about the ETF instead of a long-form prospectus. If an investor receives a summary prospectus, the ETF's long-form prospectus will be available on an Internet Web site, and an investor can obtain a paper copy upon request and without charge. Some broker-dealers also deliver a prospectus to secondary market purchasers. ETFs that do not deliver a prospectus are required to give investors a document known as a Product Description, which summarizes key information about the ETF and explains how to obtain a prospectus. All ETFs will deliver a prospectus upon request. Before purchasing ETF shares, you should carefully read all of an ETF's available information, including its prospectus.

The websites of the New York Stock Exchange and NASDAQ provide more information about different types of ETFs and how they work. An ETF will have annual operating expenses and may also impose certain shareholders fees that are disclosed in the prospectus.

Investment clubs

Investment clubs are an alternative to funds managed by professionals and as a result can keep costs down. Investment clubs are a group of private investors who pool their money and decide collectively how it should be invested. There are now well over 12,000 investment clubs in the U.K (2020). The ideal number of people in an investment club is usually between 4-20. If the membership exceeds 20 then HMRC will term the club a corporation and corporation tax will be payable. There are several stockbrokers, including major banks who have ready-made packages for investment clubs, such as Barclays and Nat West. There is a specialist charity called pro-share www.proshareclubs.co.uk which publishes a handbook on how to start an investment club. The advice contained in this handbook is very useful indeed because, although it is not absolutely necessary to have an in-depth knowledge of the stock market when joining an investment club it is at least useful to know something about the different sectors that you will be investing in.

For investors clubs there are model rules and constitutions that need to be adopted. As with all collective endeavours, from residents associations to enthusiasts clubs, rules and guidelines are essential. Investment club rules will set out, for example, how members can join and leave the club, a unit valuation system that is to be adopted, the decision making process, levels of monthly subscription, meetings, appointment of officers and so on. It is of the utmost importance that procedures are followed as disaster will almost certainly ensue. It is important to look at whether the club will run indefinitely, accumulating a portfolio or whether it has a specific life, say 5 years. An investor might be invited to join an existing club so it is important that these rules are already in place and that they are the right ones for you.

A few other tips. Only join in with people that you like and trust. Ensure that their objectives and goals are the same as yours or it could end in tears later down the line. The criteria for choosing investments varies widely from club to club but many will go for the riskier end of the market because the club membership is additional to a members own personal investments. Some investment clubs will go beyond the stock market and invest in property either directly or indirectly through another vehicle.

The main advice given to any club member or would-be member is not to invest in anything that you do not understand. Avoid the overly complex and riskier markets such as derivatives, unless you have an expert on board. Most clubs invest a small sum, it could be under £80 per month, so this type of investing is just as much fun, and social, as it is serious money making. There are some investment clubs who have had runaway success but, on the whole it is for the smaller investor with other aims in mind.

The cost of dealing in shares as an individual

Share dealing can be expensive, particularly in Britain. It is the case that it is more expensive here than in many other countries, and also the whole process is more complex, at least for individual shareholders. True, there have been moves by high street banks and other companies to make the process more transparent but it is still the case that small shareholders find the process rather confusing. It is also the case that small shareholders are still perceived to be a nuisance, because they deal in small amounts of money which cost just as much to transact as larger deals.

Commission

Commission paid to stockbrokers constitutes the main cost of dealing in shares. Commissions vary depending on the nature of the work and the type of broker. Rates of commission can vary anything from £5 per transaction up to £20 with commission on a sliding scale above the minimum depending on the value of the transaction. An order of £2,000 might cost 1.5% with the rate falling the higher the transaction. There can also be a one-off charge of at least £10 for joining Crest, the UK stock exchanges registry of share holdings. There are several internet sites, such as www.fool.co.uk which provide information about brokers commissions. It is worth looking at this site before going ahead.

The spread

As well as brokers commission there is the cost of trading. Shares are like other commodities, the costs of buying and selling shares will differ. This difference is known as the 'spread'. Spread varies with risk. Big companies listed on the FTSE 100, such as Barclays, British Airways etc have huge market capitalisations and many shareholders with regular deals every day so would have a narrow spread of say 1-1.5%. A company with few shareholders and little trade would have a spread of up to 10%. The result is that for shareholders of small companies the shares have to rise even higher to realise a profit. There is lots of free advice concerning shares. However, it is true to say that for the small, first time investor even free advice can be confusing and misleading, given that this advice is often slanted in favour of whoever gives it. It is therefore advisable to use a stockbroker who is seasoned and knows the markets well.

For those with a larger share portfolio it is possible to sub-contract out the management. The stockbroker managing the portfolio will advise on investments but leave the final decision to the investor. The value of portfolios has to be high however, and this will not usually be the route for small investors. In addition to portfolio management there is discretionary management where a fee is paid to an advisor to provide advice on shares and also the timing of share purchase. The fee paid is quite high, or is based on a percentage and is therefore only useful for those with bigger portfolios.

Income tax

When you buy shares, you usually pay a tax or duty of 0.5% on the transaction. If you buy:

- shares electronically, you'll pay Stamp Duty Reserve Tax (SDRT)
- shares using a stock transfer form, you'll pay Stamp Duty if the transaction is over £1,000

You'll have to pay tax at 1.5% if you transfer shares into some 'depositary receipt schemes' or 'clearance services'. You pay tax on the price you pay for the shares, even if their actual market value is much higher.

Transactions you pay tax on

You pay tax when you buy:

- existing shares in a company incorporated in the UK
- an option to buy shares
- an interest in shares, eg an interest in the money from selling them
- shares in a foreign company that has a share register in the UK

- rights arising from shares, eg rights you have when new shares are issued

When you don't pay tax
You don't have to pay tax if you:
- are given shares for nothing
- subscribe to a new issue of shares in a company
- buy shares in an 'open ended investment company' (OEIC) from the fund manager
- buy units in a unit trust from the fund manager

You don't normally have to pay Stamp Duty or SDRT if you buy foreign shares outside the UK. But you may have to pay other taxes.

When you sell the shares
You may need to pay Capital Gains Tax when you sell your shares.

Buying shares
The process of buying shares has become markedly easier over the last few decades. In fact, many people have acquired shares through privatisations and through building societies becoming banks, and have not had to use a stockbroker. However, if people want to buy shares in the usual way there are several routes.

The first one is finding a stockbroker. Years ago, this was out of the reach of the small investor. Most stockbrokers operated within exclusive circles. Many did not want to be bothered with the small investor who knew very little, if anything about the markets. Banks have entered the arena with share dealing services and so has a new breed of transaction only brokers (who buy and sell but do not offer advice).

However, more and more information is becoming available, through the internet and in newspapers. There has been a trend to present information in a plain English way and the information regarding shares is no different. Finding a broker over the internet is probably the easiest way to get started.

The internet has undermined the closed nature of share dealing and there are a large number of independent companies, most of which are members of The Association Of Private Client Investment Managers and Stockbrokers (see useful addresses). Many have their own web sites. There are three main types of broker, each offering a differing array of services: execution-only brokers; advisory brokers; discretionary brokers.

Execution only brokers

Execution-only brokers will simply handle the sale or purchase of shares at your request, whether this is carried out online or on the phone. They do not offer investment advice. The firms computer routes your order to the market where the shares are trading and it will simply execute your order at the best possible price. The broker will receive a commission on each transaction.

Advisory brokers

As the name suggests, an advisory broker will offer the best advice and strategies for you to increase the value of your investment portfolio and achieve your investment aims. This type of broker will try to get to know you and to gain a clearer idea of your aims. An advisory broker will be more expensive than an execution only broker, because of the more intensive nature of their service, but if you take advantage of the expert advice on offer then it will be worthwhile.

Discretionary brokers

This type of broker will have written authority from you or someone acting on your behalf to decide what securities can be bought and sold on your account.

For most new investors who may not be very knowledgeable about the markets or investing, it is generally safer to go with an advisory broker who can help you through the maze and also help to maximise the value of your investments.

People who think that they need help and advice can go to one of the big high street financial institutions with branches round the country. They can also seek out a good local firm that is experienced in the needs of small investors. The best way to find such a firm is by recommendation (like a lot of things) or you can go to the Association of Private Client Investment Managers and Stockbrokers. Before picking a broker, ask questions such as how easily contactable are they and other terms and conditions.

Internet Broking

Internet broking has, like many other activities on the internet, grown massively. The internet has a lot of real advantages. Investors can place an order whenever they feel ready and can do it from any place any time. In addition, an enormous amount of information is available online to assist with decision making.

Dealing on the internet can also be cheaper. It is possible to deal over the net for a flat fee of around £10, although this varies (see below). This is important for those who plan to be active investors and to whom the fees paid are crucial to profit margins. One Paris based research outfit called Blue Sky reckons that the four best value online brokers are all German.

The table overleaf shows 7 UK brokers with good reputations. However, there are many more brokers on the net and it is better to look around. Most banks, such as Barclays, have a share dealing service, with varied pricing.

Name	Annual fee	Frequent trader rate	Charge per trade
Halifax www.halifax.co.uk	0.5%		£12.50
Hargreaves Lansdowne www.hl.co.uk		£5.95	£11.95
Iweb www.iwebb-sharedealing.co.uk			£5
Self trade www.selftrade.co.uk		£6	£12.50
AJ Bell You Invest www.youinvest.co.uk		£4.95	£9.95
Interactive investor www.ii.co.uk		£5	£9.99
Shard Capital www.shardcapitalstockbrokers.co.uk			Varies

However, you should check the online dealers and their charges regularly.

For a periodic update go to www.money.co.uk/investing. One acknowledged problem with the web is that it is hard to get a picture of the reliability of the firm that you are dealing with.

The web is largely faceless so there are risks of various sorts, such as hacking into your data and so on. Online trading does not generate a share certificate. The shares are registered to the new owner but it is still computerised and the broker will hold the title to them in a nominee account. This can mean that the investor cannot easily change allegiance to another broker.

To join an online stockbroker, you need to get on to a website and follow instructions for registering. Almost all will require cash deposited with the brokerage. Interest is paid on this money at a low rate. When signing on you register a password which provides secure access for the investor.

United Kingdom brokers support Islamic accounts or swap-free accounts. United Kingdom Islamic accounts have no rollover interest on overnight positions to comply the Muslim faith. Traders of Islamic faith are forbidden to pay interest

If you want to invest in the US you might want to go through a US based broker. These brokers are cheaper than European counterparts.

There is a site that compares the overall performance of several online brokers, this is: www.europeaninvestor.com

There are two sorts of dealing online: one is to e-mail an instruction to a broker who will execute it via his trading screen. In theory he can do that within 15 seconds and within 15 minutes the deal can be confirmed. The other method is called real time dealing in which the investor connects directly to the stock market dealing system.

Normally, when the instruction is given, the broker will 'transact at best'-buy at the lowest available price and sell at the highest. The broker can be set a limit-the maximum at which you are prepared to buy or the minimum price below which you are not prepared to sell. Usually, such limits last for 24 hours although can be longer.

Once the transaction is complete the broker sends a contract note detailing the deal and how much money is to change hands. It may take some time to receive the share certificate but the important element is the presence on the share register.

****

Ch. 19

Spotting Financial Fraud-Different Types of Fraud And What to Look Out For.

One thing that none of us want is to lose significant amounts of hard earned money to scammers. Unfortunately, financial fraud is on the increase and it's important to be aware of the different types of fraud and where to go for help.

Pension scams

As we have discussed in the chapters covering pensions, the rules on private pensions changed in 2015, and people over 55 now have greater access to their pension pots. However, there are criminals that want to take advantage of this.

Spotting a pension scam

Fraudsters will try different ways to persuade you to part with your pension cash - from promising opportunities that are simply too good to be true, to giving you false information. They might:

- contact you out of the blue, either over the phone, text or email

- claim to know about loopholes that can help you get more than the usual 25% tax-free

- offer high returns of over 8% from overseas investments or new or creative investments

- offer a 'loan', 'saving advance' or 'cashback' from your pension
- suggest you put all your money in a single investment (in most circumstances, a financial adviser will suggest you spread your money across different schemes)
- send paperwork to your door by courier requiring an immediate signature
- say they'll help you access your pension pot before the age of 55 (unless you're seriously unwell or have a certain type of scheme, this isn't legally possible)
- pressure you into making a decision quickly
- only have a mobile phone number and/or a PO box address as contact details.

If you're planning to take your pension early, check whether there will be any penalties. If it's a workplace pension, you may need your employer's agreement to do so.

Pension scams are serious. You could lose some, if not all, your pension savings, or end up with a large tax bill (there can be high charges if you withdraw your pension savings early).cold-calling banned. Nuisance calls about pensions are now illegal. If you receive a cold call about your pension, report it to the Information Commissioner's Office on 0303 123 1113.

Avoid pension scams

If you're considering investing your pension pot, talk to an adviser regulated by the Financial Conduct Authority (FCA). Alternatively:

- Find an independent financial adviser through unbiased.co.uk

- Check the FCA's register of firms, individuals and registered businesses.
- Check the FCA's list of unauthorised firms and individuals
- Use the FCA's Warning List tool to check the risks associated with an investment opportunity

See addresses and websites at the end of the book

What to do if targeted by a pension scam

Don't be embarrassed to report a suspected pension scam, it can happen to anyone. Report it to the Information Commissioner's Office online or by calling 0303 123 1113. If you've been a victim of a scam, report it to the police and also contact Action Fraud. The information you give to Action Fraud can help track down the scammer. You can report the scam online or by calling **0300 123 2040.**

Further information

Here are some other organisations that can provide free and impartial advice.

- Unbiased.co.uk - find an independent financial adviser
- Pension wise - free guidance on pension changes

As mentioned This year, Pension Wise is being incorporated into The Money and Pensions Service www.moneyandpensionsservice.org.uk.

Doorstep scams

85% of victims of doorstep scams are aged 65 and over according to National Trading Standards. Doorstep scams take place when someone comes to your door and tries to scam you out of your money or tries to gain access to your home.

Doorstep scammers aren't always pushy and persuasive, they may seem polite or friendly. So if you're not expecting someone it's important to be vigilant when you answer the door, especially if you live on your own. It can be very easy to fall victim to a scam,

Common types of doorstep scams

There are many different types of doorstep scams, some of the most common ones include:

Rogue traders (Very common): A cold-caller may offer you a service you don't really need. They may claim to have noticed something about your property that needs work or improvement, such as the roof, and offer to fix it for cash or an inflated price.

Bogus officials: People claim to be from your utility company as a way of gaining access to your home. Always check the ID of any official, and if they're genuine they won't mind waiting while you check.

Fake charity collections: A fraudster may pretend they're from a charity and ask you to donate money, clothes or household goods. Legitimate charities will all have a charity number that can be checked on the Charity Commission website.

Made-up consumer surveys: Some scammers ask you to complete a survey so they can get hold of your personal details, or use it as a cover for persuading you to buy something you don't want or need.

Hard luck stories: Someone may come to your door and ask you to help them out with cash, ask to use your telephone or claim they're feeling unwell. The story is made up and intended to con you out of your money or gain access to your home.

Protecting yourself from doorstep scams

There are things you can do to feel safer when answering the door, such as:

Putting up a deterrent sign. You could put a 'no cold callers' sign up on your door or window, which should deter any cold callers from knocking on your door.

Setting up passwords for utilities. You can set up a password with your utility companies to be used by anyone they send round to your home. Phone your utility company to find out how to do this.

Nominating a neighbour. Find out if you have a nominated neighbour scheme where a neighbour can help to make sure if callers are safe. Contact your local Neighbourhood Watch or your local Safer Neighbourhood police team to find out more

If someone does come to the door, it's important to remember the following:

Only let someone in if you're expecting them or they're a trusted friend, family member or professional. Don't feel embarrassed about turning someone away. Don't feel pressured. Don't agree to sign a contract or hand over money at the door. Think about it and talk to someone you trust.

Check their credentials. You should always check someone's credentials - a genuine person won't mind. You can phone the company they represent or check online, but never used contact details they give you.

Don't share your PIN. Never disclose your PIN number or let anyone persuade you to hand over your bank card or withdraw cash.

Call the police. Call the police non-emergency number 101 if you're not in immediate danger but want to report an incident.

But call 999 if you feel threatened or in danger. Take the time to think about any offer, even if it's genuine. Don't be embarrassed to say 'No' to people or ask them to leave.

What should I do if I've been a victim of a doorstep scam?

Scammers are constantly finding new ways to trick people and doorstep scams are changing all the time. If you've been the victim of a scam don't be embarrassed to report it. It can happen to anyone. Report the scam to the police and contact Action Fraud. The information you give to Action Fraud can help track down the scammer.

Phone scams

Phone scams are a common way for criminals to con people out of money using various tricks to get your personal or financial information.

Cold calls

Cold calls are phone calls from companies trying to sell you something, even though they have had no business with you previously. Cold calls aren't usually illegal and don't necessarily count as a scam although they can be annoying, frustrating and even frightening. Even though it won't necessarily block scammers, you can register for free with the Telephone Preference Service (TPS) to reduce the number of cold calls you receive.

Common types of phone scams
Bank scams

In the news more frequently, someone may call claiming to be from your bank telling you there's a problem with your card or account. The caller will often sound professional and try to convince you that your card has been cloned or that your money is at risk. They may ask for your account and card details, including your PIN number, and even offer to send a courier to collect your card. They may also advise transferring your money to a 'safe account' to protect it. This is a common scam and your bank would never ask you to do this.

Computer repair scams

A scammer may call you claiming to be from the helpdesk of a well-known IT firm, such as Microsoft. They'll tell you that your computer has a virus and will ask you to download 'anti-virus software', possibly at a cost. This turns out to be spyware, used to get your personal details. Legitimate IT companies don't contact customers this way.

Compensation calls

This is a call from a company asking about a car accident you've supposedly had claiming you may be entitled to compensation. Some of these could be genuine companies looking for business but others are scammers. Don't engage in these calls. If you've had an accident, call your own insurance company on the phone number provided on your policy.

HMRC scams

You may get a call from someone claiming to be from HMRC saying there is an issue with your tax refund or an unpaid tax bill. They may leave a message and ask you to call back. Again, don't be fooled by this. HMRC would never contact you this way and would never ask you to reveal personal financial information such as your bank account details.

Number spoofing

Scammers now have the technology to mimic an official telephone number so it comes up on your caller ID display (if you have one on your phone). This can trick you into thinking the caller is really from a legitimate organisation, such as a bank or utility company. If you're in any doubt, hang up and call the organisation directly. If possible, call them from different phone as scammers can keep the phone line open, so that even if you hang up and call the organisation directly, the line may still be connected to the scammer. If it's not possible to use another phone then wait for at least 10 minutes before you call.

Pensions and investment scams

This is a call about an amazing investment opportunity, or offering you the opportunity to access your pension cash earlier. Nuisance calls about pensions are now illegal. If you receive a cold call about your pension, report it to the Information Commissioner's Office on 0303 123 1113 or go online

'Anti-scam' scams

This is a call from someone claiming to be from a charity supporting scam victims, a company selling anti-scam technology, or from someone demanding money to renew your registration, which is actually free. Be alert to all of these.

What should I do if I get a scam call?

Older people are often a target for scammers, so it's important to be aware of phone scams and how to handle them. Fortunately, there are things you can do to protect yourself:

Don't reveal personal details. Never give out personal or financial information (such as your bank account details or your

PIN) over the phone, even if the caller claims to be from your bank.

Hang up. If you feel harassed or intimidated, or if the caller talks over you without giving you a chance to speak, end the call. It may feel rude to hang up on someone, but you have the right not to be pressurised into anything.

Ring the organisation. If you're unsure whether the caller is genuine, you can always ring the company or bank they claim to be from. Make sure you find the number yourself and don't use the one provided by the caller.

Don't be rushed. Scammers will try to rush you into providing your personal details. They may say they have time-limited offer or claim your bank account is at risk if you don't give them the information they need right away.

Avoiding phone scams and cold calls

You can block or prevent some cold calls. You should:

- Register with the Telephone Preference Service – it's free and it allows you to opt out of any unsolicited live telesales calls. This should reduce the number of cold calls you receive but may not block scammers.

- Talk to your phone provider to see what other privacy services and call-blocking services are available, although you may need to pay for some of these services.

If you have a smartphone, you can use the settings on the phone to block unwanted numbers. If you're not sure how to do this, you could visit your local mobile phone shop for assistance. There are products to block some calls. Some local councils provide call blockers through their trading standards teams.

Reporting or making a complaint about a cold call?

There are privacy laws that protect consumers from direct marketing phone calls. If you've registered your phone number with the Telephone Preference Service (TPS) or if you've told the company directly that you don't wish to receive phone calls, you shouldn't receive direct marketing calls from the UK.

If you receive an unwanted telesales call, an automated message, or a spam message, tell the company that you don't wish to be contacted again. You can complain to the Information Commissioner's Office or report spam texts by forwarding the text for free to **7726**. If you have received a silent or abandoned call, complain to Ofcom www.ofcom.org.uk.

What should I do if I've been a victim of a phone scam?

If you've been the victim of a scam don't be embarrassed to report it. It can happen to anyone. Report the scam to the police and also contact Action Fraud.

What should I do next?

Register your landline and your mobile phone with the Telephone Preference Service (TPS). To register your mobile phone, text 'TPS' and your email address to 85095.

Talk to your phone provider to see what privacy services and call-blocking services are available, although you may need to pay for some of these services. Ofcom has information about different phone providers' services that block nuisance calls. If you're concerned about whether a scheme or offer is legal or legitimate, contact the Citizens Advice Consumer Service or Action Fraud for advice.

****

Association of Investment Companies (AITC)

9th Floor
24 Chiswell Street
London
EC1Y 4YY
www.theaic.co.uk
020 7282 555

Debt Management Office

UK Debt Management Office
The Minster Building
21 Mincing Lane
London
EC3R 7AG
United Kingdom
0207 862 6500
www.dmo.gov.uk

Department for Work and Pensions (DWP)

If you ring The Pension Service on 0800 731 7898,
You will be connected to the pension centre covering your area,
Or you can look on the website (www. Thepensionservice.gov.uk

Disability Action Alliance

www.disabilityactionalliance.org.uk
Provides advice and publications on social security benefits
For disabled people.

The Financial Ombudsman Service
Exchange Tower
London E14 9SR
Consumer helpline: 0800 023 4567
www.financialombudsman.org,uk

Financial Conduct Authority (FSA)
12 Endeavour Square,
London,
E20 1JN.
0800 111 6768
www.fca.gov.uk

HM Revenue & Customs (HMRC)
The government department that deals
With almost all the taxes due in the UK.
Most HMRC leaflets can be obtained
From local tax offices or Tax Enquiry Centres
(look for in the phone book under `Revenue'
or `Government Department')
or Jobcentre Plus offices.
Almost all are also available on the website at:
https://www.gov.uk/government/collections/hm-revenue-and-customs-leaflets-factsheets-and-booklets

International Pension Centre
Tel: 0191 218 7777

Moneyfacts
www.moneyfacts.co.uk

Office of the Public Guardian
The Office of the Public Guardian (OPG) protects people in England and Wales who may not have the mental capacity to make certain decisions for themselves, such as about their health and finance.
www.gov.uk/government/organisations/office-of-the-public-guardian

Pension Tracing Service
www.thepensionservice.gov.uk

Pension Advisory Service
(TPAS)
Helpline: 0800 011 3797
www.pensionsadvisoryservice.org.uk

Tax Help for Older People
Pineapple Business Park
Salway Ash
Bridport
Dorset DT6 5DB
Tel: 01308 488066 www.taxvol.org.uk

****

Index